100 Ideas for Developing

Good Practice
in the Early Years

Wendy Bowkett and
Stephen Bowkett

continuum

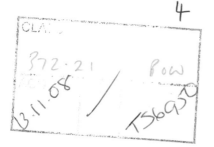
Continuum International Publishing Group

The Tower Building   80 Maiden Lane,
11 York Road   Suite 704
London   New York,
SE1 7NX   NY 10038

www.continuumbooks.com

British Library Cataloguing-in-Publication Data
A catalogue record for this book is available from the British Library.

ISBN: 9781847061669 (paperback)

Library of Congress Cataloging-in-Publication Data
Bowkett, Wendy.
  100 ideas for developing good practice in the early years / Wendy Bowkett and Stephen Bowkett.
    p. cm.
  ISBN 978-1-84706-166-9
  1. Early childhood education. 2. Early childhood teachers–In–service training. 3. Classroom management. I. Bowkett, Stephen. II. Title. III. Title: One hundred ideas for developing good practice in the early years.

  LB1139.23.B69 2008
  372.21–dc22

2008019543

Illustrations by Kerry Ingham
Illustration on page 13 by Russell Morgan
Typeset by YHT Ltd, London
Printed and bound in Great Britain by MPG Books, Cornwall

Contents

Section 3: Organization

Section 4: Social Development

Introduction

The heart of 'good practice' lies not so much in the documentation, organizational systems and physical structure of any early years setting, but rather in the people who meet, work and play there. More specifically, good practice lies with *you*, because the quality and effectiveness of an educational establishment depends essentially upon the willingness of every individual to take responsibility and show respect across the great range of situations you will experience in the course of your work.

The ideas contained in this book are all linked by those values of responsibility and respect, and empowered by the ethos of 'going beyond the given'. That is one very useful definition of creativity. We feel very strongly that good practice flourishes when individuals don't simply follow a plan or set of instructions without further thought and reflection: slavish 'teaching by numbers' will rarely bring out the best either in adults or children. Common sense is important of course, but so are spontaneity and playfulness, the ability to improvise and to exploit the educational value of what can arise, moment by moment, during any minute of any day of any week. In other words, we advocate working flexibly within the structures you inherit. Such a creative approach adds to your professionalism and keeps the work fresh and enjoyable both for you and the children. Moreover, you will be modelling a temperament that will overtly and implicitly guide the children in their own learning. When you as teacher/assistant/helper engage with the world creatively, the children are more likely to do so as well.

Gandhi once said 'be the attitude you want to see around you'. It is in this spirit that we offer the following tips, techniques and activities.

Section 1:
Overview

Adults

It's Monday. It's raining. Your weekend didn't go very well and certainly not as planned. Your journey to work has been horrendous and you get there later than you intended to. Parents and children will be arriving shortly and you've hardly got time to freshen up and grab a drink before the first session begins. The rest of the staff seem decidedly disenchanted about being there and some of them don't even manage eye-contact or even a muttered 'Good morning'. You reach your room with moments to spare. The door opens and a clutch of excited kids bundles through, closely followed by several chattering parents.

How do you react?

The answer is easy, but the (good) practice might prove more difficult. You smile, your manner is cheerful and light as though you are really looking forward to all the things you will help the children to learn about today. You greet parents and children by name and take time to exchange a few words with the adults and answer questions courteously while keeping a professionally watchful eye on the children.

Your manner, of course, has to be sincere. Children and parents will notice this and respond to it as strongly as they would if you were putting it on. Sincerity is the keyword. When you enter your work domain, leave any domestic problems behind. Set aside any differences or disagreements you may have with other staff. If one of the children played you up on Friday, welcome him today as though it had never happened. Start afresh.

Think about how a parent will view you and your place of work. Remember that your demeanour is vital. Setting your own high standards will help you to become more relaxed and self-assured, and that will have a positive influence on those around you.

IDEA 2

Children

If we had to sum up this idea in two sentences they would be 'Don't have favourites' and 'Become a camera.'

Research studies have shown repeatedly that attractive, vivacious, 'sparkly' children have more time and attention lavished upon them in schools (and elsewhere we suspect) than do their plainer, quieter, less confident contemporaries. But all children are important and all children are individuals. Again, this is an obvious thing to say, and easy to appreciate, but how do you implement the insight? It's tempting to want to interact more with lively and engaging children, and sometimes favourites develop almost without you realizing it. This is something you must be aware of, and you must make a deliberate effort to share out your time and attention equally.

But how *do* you feel about the less-advantaged child whose clothes are threadbare, who hasn't washed that morning or who has bad teeth or head-lice? It's important to be honest with yourself should you feel less inclined to want to sit close to them or tempted to be a little more dismissive when he or she asks for your attention. How you respond in light of that understanding will speak volumes about your professionalism. And, of course, however you react, your children will notice. All children are astute in this way and will pick up on both the obvious and more subliminal 'signals' you give out. So, again, what you do is helping to shape their perspective on life.

'Being a camera' means being constantly attentive to what *all* the children are doing, even as you focus your attention on one. Visually, aurally and in terms of your sixth sense, be aware of the whole room. It's commonly called having eyes in the back of your head! Another trick is to act as though you are on film. If you wouldn't like to watch it, don't do it.

IDEA 3

Buildings and rooms

Early years settings vary enormously and you may have no influence over the paintwork, décor or general state of repair of your working area. Even so, strive to ensure that your space is warm and cheerful: this is the place where the children will learn, and environment counts for a lot. Similarly, use furniture that is suitable for 'little bodies' in terms of size and cleanliness and see that your area is not cluttered or untidy. Your own standards of neatness and organization will not only make your life easier but will also have a positive knock-on effect on how the children look after the room. If tables and chairs are the wrong size, or are old and dirty, what can you do about it?

By the same token, and because individuals make up the learning community, help to make sure that all areas are supervised and that toilet areas are clean and pleasant. You may be lucky enough to have a full-time caretaker or cleaning staff always available. But, if not, what will you do if you see a dirty toilet or water splashed across the floor? If you really think that cleaning up is beneath you, you are likely to disagree with most of the ideas in this book!

The fact is, however the setting is organized, you can do something to make it better. The toilet or wet floor can't be left, and when you take responsibility and clean it up you are modelling an attitude that sets a standard you can be proud of and that the children will learn from. Responsibility and respect loop back continuously into every aspect of your good practice.

Outside play area

If you are not in charge – if you aren't the headteacher or boss – you may feel caught in a dilemma over speaking out about something that troubles you. Our advice is that it's better to voice your concerns, because if you truly have the care of the children at heart then your comments will always be justified. Part of our intention in this book is to raise your awareness (and perhaps remind more experienced colleagues) about many aspects of your role, with that very aim in mind of making yourself a more effective practitioner.

With regard to the outside play area: first and foremost, is it safe and secure? Has a member of staff gone out first to check there are no slippery fallen leaves, cat 'deposits' or other debris? Can strangers enter easily? Is somebody keeping a watchful eye on all of the children? Adequate supervision is essential, not just for this reason but in case a child falls and hurts herself or if children start to quarrel. We feel it's good practice to have staff allocated to different areas of the playground, not least because staff clumped together chatting creates a poor impression and, of course, the children are more at risk.

Depending upon the size of the play area, it may be wise to stagger playtimes to avoid overcrowding. In any case, make sure that different activities don't interfere with each other. Keep wheeled toys and ball games well separated. If a child is running after a stray ball he will most likely see nothing else and can easily run into another child on a tricycle or scooter.

In some settings equipment is available and the children are just left to use it as they please. You may want to consider some structured activities for the older children. Where else will they learn the rules of tennis, football, cricket, etc. – not to mention a sportsmanlike attitude?

A welcoming place

That your pre-school setting should be a welcoming place is an obvious point to make. If your playground is paved or surfaced with tarmac, then some tubs and pots of plants add a pleasant touch of colour, while growing herbs creates a wonderful multisensory experience. If you have a grass playground, then a flower border gives you even more scope. Get the children to help you garden. Use it as an educational opportunity to develop their observational powers. Discuss with them why plants are so named. Ask them why some plants are weeds and others aren't. Talk about the relationship between plants, insects and other creatures in the soil.

Inside the building, we feel that the vestibule (if there is one) should be bright and cheerful and not too overwhelming. Some pre-school settings bombard visitors with mission statements, welcome posters in 20 languages and inspirational quotes, which might be a little over the top. We think a lighter touch, in the form of a simple welcome notice and small tidy notice board, creates a much better impression.

Is somebody around to welcome visitors? If your setting is such that you have no receptionist then designating someone as 'welcomer' on a rota basis solves the problem. When people enter your domain, your room or area, how do you react? If you were in the parents' shoes what would make you feel welcome? A smiling, pleasant, cheerful demeanour does not have to be forced if you are truly pleased to see your visitors. Be proud of the place. And, if you aren't (yet), then ask yourself why, and do something about it.

IDEA 6

Questions to ask yourself

In our opinion, constant self-evaluation is a hallmark of good practice. By this we don't mean forever finding fault with yourself, or even assuming that you have to improve in all areas. Recognizing that you have done something well and being duly pleased with yourself is also very important. Similarly, if you have a good idea or useful insight, then share it with your colleagues so that it can be more widely implemented.

Endeavour to see things from other people's points of view. If you were a parent, for example, these questions might well be among the ones you ask:

● Do the staff seem happy, motivated and enthusiastic?

● Are the staff qualified and experienced? Are there in-house and/or external training programmes to augment the practitioners' experience?

● Are the children getting individual attention? Are the children being treated equally in this way?

● Are the buildings and outside areas secure?

● Are rooms clean and well kept? Is there an atmosphere of calm, well-organized activity?

● Do the children appear happy, settled and busy? Is the 'busyness' productive, or are the children milling around rather aimlessly?

● Is there a balance between structured activity and opportunities for play?

Questions from the practitioner's point of view:

● How do you see your role in the setting? By this we mean not just whether you encourage and guide the children in their learning, but also do you proactively strive to improve your workplace in a variety of ways?

● What are your good qualities, and do you use them positively in your work?

● Do some children respond to you more positively than others? Why might this be so?

- If you are unsure about anything, do you ask?

In summary, if you aren't self-aware you won't improve as quickly. And if you don't act or speak out the situation is not likely to improve.

Section 2:
Creating the Ethos

Setting high standards for yourself

The word 'ethos' comes from the Greek, meaning 'character' and 'custom'. The character of any setting is a complex interaction between the environment – the building, the layout of rooms and the organizational structures that exist – and the people who work and learn there. Some aspects of the ethos of a place are obvious and can be changed, but others are more subtle and amount to a vague feeling or a 'vibe' that's picked up subliminally as you absorb the atmosphere. Think back to places (early years settings or otherwise) that gave you that 'gut reaction'. Perhaps you found one to be warm and friendly, or another to be coldly formal? If you are currently working in a pre-school setting, how would you describe its ethos?

Any ethos, good or bad, is powerfully influenced by the headteacher or boss. Either way, you can make a difference by setting your own high standards. We feel that in practice this means taking the initiative as an individual when this is appropriate, but also working as part of the team or 'learning community'.

Thinking as an individual means taking action for yourself. Just because there are many adults around don't assume that someone else will solve the problem or deal with the situation. If, for instance, you see some litter in the corridor, picking it up yourself and not leaving it for someone else to do is an example of the high standards we're talking about. On the other hand, if something needs attending to that can't be fixed by you alone, then mention it to the 'powers-that-be'. Another important aspect of your personal standard is not to try to take on everything yourself. Use the team. Ask your colleagues for help and advice when this is needed.

IDEA 8

Showing by example

When you set high standards for yourself, showing by example becomes a powerful and positive influence on children's learning (and sometimes that of other adults too!). At the heart of this lie the qualities we've already mentioned, namely responsibility and respect, coupled with a certain degree of assertiveness that grows out of self-confidence. In turn, self-confidence increases as a result of your intention to set high personal standards. It's a positive feedback loop.

Whatever standards you establish for yourself, you will need to work within the setting's framework of rules. In an educational system that many argue has become bogged down by the imposition of too many rules, there are nevertheless certain precepts and principles that remain useful. The notion of consistency is important here. If there is a rule which says 'Don't run down the corridor', what do you do if a child who's desperate to use the toilet starts to run down the corridor? What do you do if you hear a child cry out in a room at the other end of the hall?

The fact is that knowing the limits of what's allowed is part of the children's learning, and while it's sometimes easier just to let things go by, that results in a general lowering of standards that will cause problems later.

One issue you might encounter is where other colleagues and/or the management don't set the same high standards as you do or follow the established rules of the setting. In other words, there is no consistency of practice and it's 'Do as I say not as I do' as far as the children are concerned.

How could you deal with this? Read on!

IDEA

9

Expressing your thoughts and ideas

You can of course follow your own 'treat someone as you would like to be treated' policy, regardless of what's going on around you. This, at least, means that you are being true to yourself. But you might also tactfully raise the matter at a staff gathering. Putting this in the form of a general question avoids pointing the finger at anyone in particular. If the issue is about the use of good manners, you can approach it by saying, 'We expect the children to say "please" and "thank you", but do we always do it?' Or, 'I've noticed that [a child] doesn't say "please" or "thank you" very much. What do you think we could all do to improve that situation?'

However, be prepared for backlash in the form of negative responses, assumptions, judgements and generalizations. One colleague might reply, 'Well, when you look at his parents what can you expect?' Or, 'Even if he said it he wouldn't mean it, so what's the point?' How could you respond positively to this? How would you feel about this whole issue if senior management didn't usually say 'please' and 'thank you'?

It's quite likely that in your work situation you will meet widely differing standards and encounter clashing personalities. Sometimes, alas, this makes for problems that are insoluble. If progress really can't be made, bear these points in mind:

- Remember that you are responsible for what you say, but not for what other people hear and think.

- Value your personal integrity and strive to maintain your own high standards.

- If self-confidence is a problem for you, consider some assertiveness training. Assertiveness means speaking out in a firm, friendly and considered way.

- Follow Dr Deepak Chopra's advice: How to be happy? Stop having opinions.

- Don't take work-related problems home with you.

IDEA 10

The danger of making judgements

A wise old saying is that good judgement comes from experience – and experience comes from bad judgement. That's true if we learn from our bad judgements, but unfortunately this does not always happen, either with children or adults. It's very easy to come to a judgement that has not been considered or is the result of peer pressure. Peer pressure is a powerful force on people of all ages and it is all too easy to absorb opinions and prejudices not because you want to, or feel them to be right, but because they help you to belong to the group.

Setting one's own high standards, working professionally and with integrity, begins by noticing one's own thoughts and reactions and how these can sometimes be the precursors to jumping to conclusions, making assumptions and generalizing. In other words, catch your mind in action and reflect upon what you are doing. This is an important aspect of *metacognition*, thinking about the thinking you do, and it lies at the heart of all true learning.

Look at the picture opposite. It is called *Family*. What thoughts immediately spring to mind? What is your impression of the man? What reaction do you have to the child? What do you think about the woman? What evidence do you have for any of these opinions? The more you catch your mind in action, the more effectively you can choose to react differently.

Simon Winston, a survivor of the Holocaust, makes the point that unconsidered reactions and the passive acceptance of others' opinions leads to generalizations, then prejudice, then hatred. He makes a direct link between individual 'isms' and those held by one race or creed about another. The power of Simon's message is that because it starts with individuals it can end with individuals. And when you are aware of how you make judgements, you can pass your learning on to the children.

IDEA

11

Playroom scenarios

A useful workshop for staff is to set up a playroom so that it contains a number of faults or dangers that your colleagues then have to notice. Every room is different of course, but some of the things you might stage are:

- leaving scissors lying around

- a water-spill on the floor

- glue containers with missing tops

- a staple gun within reach of children

- an air freshener within reach

- books piled unsafely within reach

- small items – building-bricks, toys, etc. – lying about.

Even just thinking about this activity is good practice for creating a safer environment!

IDEA 12

Your creative attitude

We decided not to let children play with guns or militaristic toys at our nursery. Even so, we often found that both boys and girls made very sword- or gun-like shapes out of Lego, sticklebricks, cardboard tubes, etc. On being challenged about this children would say things like 'No, it's only a water pistol', or 'It's a magic wand', or even 'Yes, but I know it's not a real gun.'

Deep down we appreciated this, because it was an example of the creative attitude that all children have, but which sometimes develops in only a minority. A central principle of the creative attitude is to 'go beyond the given'. In other words, to make something more out of what's already there. As we have said previously (and will say again) your attitude influences the children.

Take something and make it into something else. A piece of card can become a mask or a spy-hole. Use it as a pinhole camera to project the image of the sun (any good basic book of astronomy will tell you how to do this). Use a pegboard for threading activities, or as an abacus for counting. Peg out beads to create rainbows and to illustrate symmetry.

Try tearing up tissue paper instead of cutting with scissors to make shapes for use in a story or rhyme (which you can make up) or to use as simple colour filters. Open a book and stand it to make a tunnel, or garage, or engine shed. Use books to illustrate the idea that size and weight are not directly connected. Crumple a blanket to make a landscape, use a cushion to make hills, or tinfoil to make a lake.*

So, go beyond the given. The more you do it, the more you verify for the children that it's fine for them to be like that too.

* For more ideas see our *100 Ideas for Creative Development in the Early Years* (London: Continuum, 2008).

IDEA 13

Time-filling or learning?

There will be many occasions when children finish a set activity at different times and the ones who finish first will have minutes to spare. What might you do to help them fill that time usefully, to give it *learning value*? Building a repertoire of filler activities that you can justify educationally is part of your good practice. Here are a few ideas that worked for us:

- Colouring by numbers. This develops hand–eye coordination and fine motor skills while building an awareness of control (over the pencils). It gives children practice in number recognition and cross-linking numbers to colour. It aids concentration. As a child completes one section of colour she experiences an ongoing sense of achievement. The whole activity is enjoyable – and in our opinion enjoyment is always educationally worthwhile!

- Threading buttons, beads, etc. on to a lace. This develops concentration also and pattern-recognition at a fine level of detail. There is a strong creative element in encouraging children to vary your pattern or create one of their own. Threading boosts perception skills and visual memory. The completed work gives children a vital sense of ownership of their ideas and a sense of mastery over a skill.

- A box of matchsticks, lollipop sticks, etc. Children use these to make shapes and patterns. The creative element is strong here too. Choice and decision-making are encouraged while concentration and manual dexterity are developed.

The famous educationalist Maria Montessori always had little baskets and trays of things for the children to do, such as button-fastening, shells and pebbles to hold and touch, spooning beads from one bowl to another. In light of what you've read, what learning value do these have?

Remember that your guided stimulation will stop children being bored, and boredom is anathema to learning.

IDEA 14

A clear sense of purpose

Keeping a variety of activities in your mind for filling spare moments valuably shows a clear sense of pedagogic purpose. Knowing plenty of songs, rhymes and stories are obvious examples. As children finish a set task, tidy up and begin to gather them round you – start up a clapping game or a group poem they can join in with. Provide a box for children to put the teddies, cars and toys they bring to pre-school. Use this to involve children who are 'at a loose end' until the next session, playtime, mealtime, etc. begins. Take an item out of the box and say 'Now don't tell me who brought this in today, let's see if the rest of us can guess.' Or take items out one by one and encourage the children to help you make up a story that features them.

Don't waste moments. Instead of children just standing around lining up, or if outside play is cancelled due to bad weather, do some loosening-up exercises or play the 'Simon Says' game to keep them busy. Obviously there will be constraints in some early years settings. Maybe you don't have much floor space – in which case, using your clear sense of purpose, what ideas can you think of now?

IDEA 19

Naming and complimenting

Our names are usually precious to us and form an important part of our identity. To use someone's name immediately creates a powerful link between you. This is an obvious thing to say of course. No less obvious is to greet the children by name as they arrive in your room. This tells them that you have noticed them and acknowledge their presence. It is so much warmer and friendlier than the mechanical registrations they have to endure for the rest of their schooling.

Combining your greeting with a compliment makes the child feel even more special. Wendy would often try to meet new arrivals at the door and typically might say 'Good morning Lucy – oh, I like the dress you're wearing today.' Lucy would feel pleased and often make a point of showing Wendy her shoes as well. Sometimes – just like us – children don't have a good start to the day. Maybe there was a disagreement at home, or perhaps mum or dad was in a bad mood on the journey to playgroup or school. Naming and complimenting is an effective way of changing what could be a negative emotional state in the child. If lots of children are arriving at once, arrange a group gathering where you notice and speak to the children you haven't complimented yet. They will certainly notice if you don't!

However, your praise has to be sincere. False flattery is usually recognized as such and has the opposite effect to what you intended. More broadly, sincerely highlighting the positive is a powerful counterbalance to the often negatively corrective ethos children usually have to cope with throughout their school lives.

IDEA
20

Freedom to choose, explore and imagine

There is a wise old saying in the world of education which goes 'I hear and I forget, I see and I remember, I do and I understand.' Learning by doing is one of the most effective educational strategies that exist. And because children naturally have what has been called *insistent curiosity* they are usually motivated to choose, explore and imagine within the context for learning that you offer them.

Of course, there is not time to allow children to 'rediscover the wheel' in every case. Because the National Curriculum is all about 'coverage', sometimes you simply have to tell the children about things, and in a limited time-frame at that. One effective compromise is to use *the principle of the controlled accident*. This simply means that you set up your session in such a way that children are almost guaranteed to make the discoveries that constitute the learning you want them to have.

One example is when Wendy was doing a session on colour lenses. She had deliberately put out certain colours on the tables and asked the children to 'play' with them – i.e. experiment. It wasn't long before Samantha superimposed a yellow lens over a red one and found that made orange. She was immediately very excited about this and rushed over to tell Wendy, who asked her to show the other children what she had just learned, thus ensuring that Samantha felt proud as well as pleased. And although the other children had not made that discovery for themselves, they saw very clearly how to combine colours to make new ones.

Leonardo da Vinci said that all true knowledge arises from one's own direct experience. Providing those experiences lies at the heart of education.

IDEA
21

Remembering, embedding and ownership

Many years ago the novelist Aldous Huxley wrote an essay pointing out the fragmented nature of the Western educational system, which focuses on the mental accumulation of facts and measures students' success by how many of those facts they can reiterate under formal conditions – that is, how well they can pass exams by recalling the 'right answers'. Nothing seems to have changed in the decades since then.

Other cultures look at learning differently. The scientist F. David Peat (in *Blackfoot Physics**) talks about how Native American peoples view education as a process he describes as 'coming-to-knowing', where understanding is acquired through direct experience and a relationship with the thing to be known. Simply put, it's the difference between trying to explain to a child what salt tastes like and giving him some salt to taste. The power of the learning is in the doing.

Steve remembers sitting in on an ICT lesson once where, for 50 minutes, the teacher talked about computers while all around the children computer screens were blank (as were the faces of many of the children), and not one child got to lay his hands on a keyboard! In contrast to that, at our after-school club 6-year-old Leo showed us things about computers that we never knew before. When we asked him how he had learned all this stuff he said 'Just by playing about to see what happened.' His coming-to-knowing had been very effective indeed.

Repeated direct experience *embeds* knowledge and understanding. It becomes a part of us. The philosopher Michael Polyani calls this *tacit knowledge*. We come to know it not by verbal instruction but by engaging with whatever it is to be mastered. How do we learn to ride a bicycle? And as everybody knows, once you can ride one you never forget how to do it.

* F. David Peal, *Blackfoot Physics* (Newbury Port, MA: Weiser, 2006).

IDEA 22

Self-endeavour and competition

The 'accumulation of facts' model of education usually goes hand-in-hand with an ethos of competition, where predefined standards are imposed upon the learning environment. When children attain these standards they have succeeded, and unfortunately, if they don't attain them, they have not – they have failed. Years ago there used to be the 'ladder' metaphor of attainment. There was the top of the class, the bottom of the class and all the rungs in between. Some teachers would rank children in this crude way based on tests and pin up the list on the noticeboard!

We feel that things have not changed that much. In a world of levels, goals and targets, children are still under pressure to reach a certain rung by a given time in their lives. Children are also often measured one against another, so that no matter how hard Jack tries, if he doesn't reach the same level as Jill he has not done as well.

Sometimes the strategy of competitiveness is useful and positive. In certain contexts, sport for instance, pitting yourself against others can bring out the best in you. The ethos here is not bluntly about winning or losing (though it's often viewed as such), but rather about the achievement of taking part and giving your all. The success is in the trying to improve.

We believe that what links competitiveness in sport with children's learning is the urge to *self-endeavour* – the 'attempt to do', which develops initiative, independence and resilience in the learner.

This idea works well in many ways. We remember Simon, a very angry boy, who through his own endeavours learned to control his temper (most of the time). Sometimes he tried so hard not to have an outburst, and we always praised him for that. Comparing him with Andrew, who was always placid, would have done Simon no good at all.

Lower of cost and NRV rule

The rules for valuing inventory come from IAS 2 The basic rule for valuation is:

Inventory should be valued at the lower of COST and NET REALISABLE VALUE.

Before we look at what is included in these two figures we will consider the purpose of this rule.

It is based upon the accounting concept of **prudence**, which we saw in Chapter 2. The normal situation is that an item will be purchased for say £30 and then resold for £40. In this case the inventory will be valued at cost of £30. However, suppose the item could only be sold for £25. If we valued it at £30 we would be overstating its value as an asset. The prudence concept does not allow this so the item must be valued at its selling price of £25.

So what are cost and net realisable value?

- IAS 2 states that cost comprises 'all costs of purchase, costs of conversion and other costs incurred in bringing the items to their present location and condition'.

- NET REALISABLE VALUE is the expected selling price of the inventory, less any further costs to be incurred such as selling or distribution costs. IAS 2 defines it as 'the estimated selling price in the ordinary course of business less the estimated costs of completion and the estimated costs necessary to make the sale'.

Task 1

A product that a business sells costs £13.80 to buy. Due to a fall in demand for this product it will only sell for £14.00 and in order to sell at this price it must be delivered to the customer at a cost of 50p per unit.

At what value should inventory of this product be included in the financial statements?

£ _____

HOW IT WORKS

A small business has three lines of inventory A, B and C. The total cost and total net realisable value (NRV) of each line is given below:

	Cost	NRV
	£	£
A	1,250	2,000
B	1,400	1,200
C	1,100	1,900
	3,750	5,100

Although the total cost of £3,750 is lower than the total net realisable value of £5,100 this is not the value of the business's closing inventory. The cost and net realisable value must be compared for each individual line of inventory as follows:

	Cost	NRV	Lower = Inventory value
	£	£	£
A	1,250	2,000	1,250
B	1,400	1,200	1,200
C	1,100	1,900	1,100
	3,750	5,100	3,550

The inventory should be valued at £3,550 which is the total of the lower of cost and net realisable value for each line.

METHODS OF DETERMINING COST

Before they can apply the cost/NRV rule, businesses are often faced with the problem of determining the actual cost price of the items held. If there are deliveries and issues of an item on a regular basis then it will be difficult (if not impossible) to determine precisely which items have been sold and which remain as the closing inventory. If the prices at which each batch of the item was purchased differ then it becomes important that we know which purchases remain in inventory at the end of the accounting period.

The time and effort involved in determining exactly which item has been sold and exactly which remains in inventory will usually not be worthwhile for a business. Therefore the cost of inventory will be determined by using one of a number of assumptions as follows:

BPP
LEARNING MEDIA

- **FIFO (FIRST IN FIRST OUT)** we assume that the items issued are the earliest purchases, so the inventory on hand comprise the most recent purchases.

- **LIFO (LAST IN FIRST OUT)** we assume that the items issued are the most recent purchases, so the items in inventory are the earliest purchases. Some businesses will use this method for day-to-day stock control in practice but IAS 2 forbids it.

- **AVCO (WEIGHTED AVERAGE COST)** after each new purchase a weighted average cost for the items held is calculated – this is the total cost of the items held divided by the number of units held – the inventory is valued at this weighted average at the end of the period.

HOW IT WORKS

Dawn Fisher's stores record for extra small white T shirts for March is shown below.

White T shirt – extra small   **Code 01335**

Date	Purchases	Issues	Balance
1 Mar	Balance b/d		140
15 Mar		80	60
27 Mar	100		160
28 Mar		40	120

The 140 items held on 1 March were all purchased at £7 per unit, and the purchase on 27 March was at £8 per unit.

The value of the 120 units remaining in inventory at the end of the month will be calculated on the FIFO, LIFO and AVCO basis.

FIFO – First in first out

Date	Purchases units	Cost/ unit £	Issues units	Cost/ unit £	Total units	Cost/ units £	Total cost £
1 Mar (b/d)					140	7.00	980.00
15 Mar			(80)		(80)	7.00	(560.00)
27 Mar	100	8.00			100	8.00	800.00
28 Mar			(40)		(40)	7.00	(280.00)
					120		940.00

LIFO – Last in first out

Date	Purchases units	Cost/ unit £	Issues units	Cost/ unit £	Total units	Cost/ Units £	Total cost £
1 Mar (b/d)					140	7.00	980.00
15 Mar			(80)		(80)	7.00	(560.00)
27 Mar	100	8.00			100	8.00	800.00
28 Mar			(40)	8.00	(40)	8.00	(320.00)
					120		900.00

AVCO – Weighted average cost

Date	Purchases quantity	Cost per unit £	Issues units	Cost per unit £	Balance Units	£
1 Mar Bal b/d	140	7.00		7.00	140	980.00
15 Mar			(80)	7.00	(80)	(560.00)
27 Mar	100	8.00		8.00	100	800.00
	Av. cost	1,220/160		7.625	160	1,220.00
28 Mar			(40)	7.625	(40)	(305.00)
					120	915.00

As you can see the values of the inventory under the different methods vary:

	£
FIFO	940.00
LIFO	900.00
AVCO	915.00

Task 2

A business buys 100 units of a product for £3.50 per unit on 1 May. A further 100 units are purchased on 20 May for £4.00 per unit. The sales for the month were 70 units on 12 May and 80 units on 30 May.

Determine the value of the closing inventory using the FIFO method.

£ [   ]

LEDGER ACCOUNTING FOR INVENTORY

Whenever goods are purchased they must be debited to a purchases account, **never** to an inventory account. The inventory account is only used at the end of the accounting period in order to record the closing inventory of the business.

HOW IT WORKS

Dawn Fisher has counted and valued all of her inventory at her year end 31 March 20X5 and it totals £6,450.

This figure is entered into the ledger accounts by a debit and a credit entry to two different inventory accounts:

Debit   Inventory account – statement of financial position
Credit Inventory account – statement of profit or loss

Inventory account – statement of financial position

	£		£
31 Mar 20X5	6,450		

Inventory account – statement of profit or loss

	£		£
		31 Mar 20X5	6,450

The inventory - statement of financial position account balance, a debit balance, is the closing inventory asset that will be listed in the statement of financial position as a current asset.

The inventory - statement of profit or loss balance is cleared out to the statement of profit or loss at the end of the year, to be shown eventually as a deduction from purchases to give the cost of sales figure.

Inventory account – statement of profit or loss

	£		£
31 Mar 20X5 SPL	6,450	31 Mar 20X5	6,450

Dawn's purchases account at the end of the year shows a debit balance of £76,850. This is also cleared to the statement of profit or loss for the year. We deduct the inventory account – statement of profit or loss balance to arrive at the figure for cost of sales:

	£
Cost of sales as at 31 March 20X5:	
Purchases	76,850
Less: closing inventory	(6,450)
	70,400

The only inventory balance that remains in Dawn's books now is that on the inventory – statement of financial position account. This remains in her ledger accounts as the opening inventory balance without any further entries to it until the end of the following accounting period, 31 March 20X6. At this date the closing inventory is valued at £7,200 and the purchases for the year were £80,900.

As this is Dawn's second year we have both opening and closing inventory.

Step 1   At 31 March 20X6, clear the balance on the inventory account (which is the opening inventory), to the statement of profit or loss.

Inventory account – statement of financial position

	£		£
1 Apr 20X5 Bal b/d	6,450	31 Mar 20X6 SPL	6,450
Opening inventory			

Step 2   Enter the closing inventory valuation at 31 March 20X6 into the two inventory accounts:

Inventory account – statement of financial position

	£		£
		31 Mar 20X6 SPL	6,450
1 Apr 20X5 Bal	6,450		
b/d Opening			
inventory			
31 Mar 20X6	7,200		
Closing inventory			

Inventory account – statement of profit or loss

	£		£
		31 Mar 20X6 Closing	7,200
		inventory	

Step 3   Clear the account for inventory – statement of profit or loss to the statement of profit or loss as the closing inventory:

Inventory account – statement of profit or loss

	£		£
31 Mar 20X6 SPL	7,200	31 Mar 20X6 Closing	7,200
		inventory	

Step 4   Calculate the cost of sales in the statement of profit or loss for the year ended 31 March 20X6:

	£
Cost of sales as at 31 March 20X6:	
Opening inventory	6,450
Purchases	80,900
	87,350
Less: closing inventory	(7,200)
	80,150

Journal entry for recording closing inventory

The journal entry with narrative for recording the closing inventory for Dawn Fisher would be as follows:

Account name	Debit £	Credit £
Inventory account – statement of financial position	7,200	
Inventory account – statement of profit or loss		7,200

Being inventory held at 31 March 20X6

To summarise:

Statement of profit or loss

- Debit with opening inventory
- Credit with closing inventory

Statement of financial position

- Debit with closing inventory as a current asset

This may seem complicated now but when we start dealing with the extended trial balance it will become second nature!

Task 3

When goods are purchased the cost should be debited to which ledger account:

	✓
Inventory	
Purchases	

CHAPTER OVERVIEW

- When goods are purchased they are always debited to a purchases account and never to an inventory account

- At the end of the year, and often at other times during the year, the inventory must be counted and the quantity of each item listed – this is then compared to the stores record of the amount of that item that should exist – an inventory reconciliation will be carried out

- Once the quantity of each item of inventory is known then it must be valued – both SSAP 9 and IAS 2 state that each line of inventory should be valued at the lower of cost and net realisable value (NRV)

- In order to determine the cost of inventory a method has to be chosen – the most common methods are FIFO, LIFO (not permitted under IAS 2) and AVCO (weighted average cost)

- When the closing inventory has been valued it must be included in the final accounts as a current asset in the statement of financial position and as a deduction from purchases to give cost of sales in the statement of profit or loss

- Opening inventory for a period is included as an expense in the statement of profit or loss, being added to the purchases figure in the cost of sales calculation

Keywords

Inventory count – the regular and year end process of counting each line of inventory and comparing the quantity to the quantity that should exist according to the stores records

Closing inventory reconciliation – comparison of inventory record quantity to quantity actually counted

Cost – the cost for inventory is the cost of getting the inventory to its current position which will include delivery costs

Net realisable value (NRV) – the expected selling price of the item less any further costs to be incurred such as selling or distribution expenses

FIFO – first in first out – method of inventory valuation that assumes that items issued are the earliest purchases so closing inventory contains the most recent purchases

LIFO – last in first out – method of inventory valuation that assumes that the items issued are the most recent purchases so closing inventory contains the earliest purchases

AVCO – weighted average cost – method of inventory valuation that operates by calculating a weighted average cost for the inventory after each new purchase

TEST YOUR LEARNING

Test 1

A business has 120 units of an item at the year end which cost £25.80 plus delivery charges of £1.00 per unit. This item can be sold for £28.00 per unit but must be delivered to the customer at a further cost of £1.10 per unit.

(a) The cost of each item is £ ☐ and the net realisable value of each item is £ ☐ .

(b) At what value would these 120 units appear in the statement of financial position?

£ ☐

chapter 8:
IRRECOVERABLE DEBTS AND DOUBTFUL DEBTS

— chapter coverage 📖 —

In this chapter we consider the receivables balance at the end of the accounting year and any adjustments that are required. The topics we cover are:

- ✍ Introduction to irrecoverable debts
- ✍ Accounting for irrecoverable debts
- ✍ Accounting for irrecoverable debts recovered
- ✍ Introduction to doubtful debts
- ✍ Accounting for doubtful debts
- ✍ Specific and general allowances for doubtful debts
- ✍ Adjusting the allowance for doubtful debts

INTRODUCTION TO IRRECOVERABLE DEBTS

When a sale is made on credit it is recognised immediately in the accounting records by recording it as a sale and setting up a receivable for the amount due – this is in accordance with the **accruals** concept. We expect the debt to be honoured and the amount paid by the customer. However, it is possible that some debts may never be paid so, in line with the **prudence** concept and to avoid any overstatement of assets, any debts that are unlikely to be paid should not be shown as an asset in the statement of financial position.

An IRRECOVERABLE DEBT is one that the business believes will never be paid (you may sometimes hear it being referred to as a 'bad debt').

ACCOUNTING FOR IRRECOVERABLE DEBTS

If a debt is not going to be recovered then it should be removed from the business's accounts and it should not be shown as a receivable in the statement of financial position.

The double entry for this is:

Debit Irrecoverable debts expense account
Credit Sales ledger control account

This will remove the debt from the receivables balance and create an expense – irrecoverable debts expense – in the statement of profit or loss.

The customer's individual account in the sales ledger must also have the debt removed from it by a credit entry here as well.

HOW IT WORKS

The balance on Dawn Fisher's sales ledger control account at the year end date of 31 March 20X5 is £10,857. She is however very concerned about an amount of £337 owing from K Whistler. The last money received from this customer was in September 20X4 and Dawn's latest letter has been returned unopened with a scribbled comment on the envelope 'K Whistler not known at this address'. Dawn has now decided to accept that the debt will never be paid and is to write it off as irrecoverable.

Irrecoverable debts expense account

Date	Details	£	Date	Details	£
31 Mar	Sales ledger control	337			

Sales ledger control account

Date	Details	£	Date	Details	£
31 Mar	Balance b/d	10,857	31 Mar	Irrecoverable debts expense	337
			31 Mar	Balance c/d	10,520
		10,857			10,857
1 Apr	Balance b/d	10,520			

The sales ledger control account now shows the amended balance of £10,520 after having removed K Whistler's debt. The irrecoverable debts expense account has a debit balance of £337 which is an expense of the business, one of the risks of making sales on credit, and as such will be charged in the statement of profit or loss as an expense.

In the sales ledger K Whistler's account must also be credited with the amount of this irrecoverable debt to remove it from these records as well:

K Whistler

Date	Details	£	Date	Details	£
31 Mar	Balance b/d	337	31 Mar	Irrecoverable debt written off	337

Task 1

A business has receivables at the year end of £26,478. Of these it is felt that £976 should be written off as irrecoverable.

What is the journal entry, including narrative, for the write-off of these irrecoverable debts?

Account name	Debit £	Credit £

ACCOUNTING FOR IRRECOVERABLE DEBTS RECOVERED

Occasionally a debt will be settled by a customer after it has been written off by the business as irrecoverable.

The double entry for this requires the expense of the write-off to be removed from the irrecoverable debts account – as it has already been written off there is no adjustment to the sales ledger control account:

    Debit   Bank/cash account
    Credit Irrecoverable debts expense account

Task 2

A business has written off a debt for £1,000 from one of its customers and then three months later the amount is received.

Prepare the journal entry, including narrative, to record the recovery.

Account name	Debit £	Credit £

INTRODUCTION TO DOUBTFUL DEBTS

We have seen that an irrecoverable debt is one that we are fairly sure will never be recovered. There may also be other debts that we are concerned about but that we are not yet ready to write off as irrecoverable. Our concern may arise from a customer querying an amount or not responding to initial requests for payment of an overdue debt.

These debts over which there is some concern are known as DOUBTFUL DEBTS.

There is also another scenario with customers owing money. A business may not necessarily be able to pinpoint specific debts that are doubtful but the sales ledger clerk may know from experience that, on average, a certain percentage of debts turn out to be doubtful. In this case the percentage can be applied to the total receivables figure to give an indication of the amount of doubtful debts.

ACCOUNTING FOR DOUBTFUL DEBTS

According to the **prudence** concept if there is uncertainty as to the recoverability of debts then there is a possibility that an asset – receivables – will be overstated in the statement of financial position. While we need to include the most cautious figure for assets in the statement of financial position, we do not want to remove these debts from the sales ledger control account since they may well yet be recovered, unlike an irrecoverable debt. Consequently, we set up an ALLOWANCE FOR DOUBTFUL DEBTS.

An allowance is a ledger account with a credit balance which is deducted (or 'netted off') against an asset ledger account when the statement of financial position is prepared. The allowance for doubtful debts account is similar therefore to the accumulated depreciation account. On the statement of financial position this is presented as a depreciation balance that is deducted from the non-current assets at cost balance in order to arrive at their carrying amount.

In a similar way the allowance for doubtful debts is a credit balance which is deducted from the sales ledger control account balance to show the net figure for receivables that are recoverable in the statement of financial position. It is a less permanent way of achieving the prudent figure for receivables than writing the debt out of the sales ledger control account as an irrecoverable debt.

Double entry to set up an allowance for doubtful debts

The double entry to set up an allowance for doubtful debts is:

Debit   Allowance for doubtful debts adjustment account
Credit   Allowance for doubtful debts account

The ALLOWANCE FOR DOUBTFUL DEBTS ADJUSTMENT ACCOUNT is an expense account that will have a debit balance when an allowance is first set up.

SPECIFIC AND GENERAL ALLOWANCES FOR DOUBTFUL DEBTS

We have seen that there are potentially two types of doubtful debt – the specific debts that can be pinpointed as doubtful and the more general percentage approach.

This means that a business could have a policy of having two elements to its allowance for doubtful debts:

- A SPECIFIC ALLOWANCE
- A GENERAL ALLOWANCE

HOW IT WORKS

Dawn Fisher's balance on her sales ledger control account at 31 March 20X5 after writing off the irrecoverable debt from K Whistler is £10,520.

When Dawn considers these debts in detail she decides that she is concerned about the recoverability of one debt for £320. She has also been advised by friends in business that she is likely to have problems on average with about 2% of her receivables.

Therefore Dawn's policy is to set up an allowance for doubtful debts made up of two elements:

- A specific allowance for £320
- A general allowance of 2% of the remaining balance of receivables

Step 1 Calculate the total amount of the allowance. Before applying a percentage to the sales ledger control account total to calculate a general allowance you should always deduct:

- Any irrecoverable debts that are to be written off
- Any debts against which a specific allowance is to be made

	£
Sales ledger control account balance after writing off irrecoverable debts	10,520
Specific allowance	(320)
	10,200
General allowance 2% × £10,200	204
Specific allowance	320
Amount of allowance to be set up	524

Step 2 Enter the allowance into the ledger accounts.

Allowance for doubtful debts adjustment account

Date	Details	£	Date	Details	£
31 Mar	Allowance for doubtful debts	524	31 Mar	SPL	524
		524			524

Allowance for doubtful debts

Date	Details	£	Date	Details	£
			31 Mar	Allowance for doubtful debts adjustment	524

Step 3 Close off the balance on the allowance for doubtful debts adjustment account of £524 to the statement of profit or loss as an expense.

Step 4 When Dawn produces her statement of financial position the sales ledger control account balance will have the allowance deducted from it to show the figure for receivables that are truly recoverable:

	£
Sales ledger control account	10,520
Less: allowance for doubtful debts account	(524)
Receivables figure in the statement of financial position	9,996

Task 3

A business has a sales ledger control account balance of £21,680. One debt of £680 is to be written off as irrecoverable and an allowance of 3% is to be made against the remainder.

Prepare the journal entries, including narrative, to record the irrecoverable debt and the allowance being set up.

Account name	Debit £	Credit £

ADJUSTING THE ALLOWANCE FOR DOUBTFUL DEBTS

In subsequent years the balance on the allowance for doubtful debts account will remain in the ledger accounts as it is a statement of financial position account, but it may require increasing or decreasing each year.

To increase the allowance for doubtful debts the double entry is:

Debit   Allowance for doubtful debts adjustment account
Credit   Allowance for doubtful debts account

- With the amount of the increase required

To decrease the allowance for doubtful debts the double entry is:

Debit   Allowance for doubtful debts account
Credit   Allowance for doubtful debts adjustment account

- With the amount of the decrease required

HOW IT WORKS

A business has a policy of providing against 4% of its receivables at the year end. Its sales ledger control account balance at 31 December 20X6, the end of its first year of trading, was £24,000 after writing off irrecoverable debts of £200. At the end of 20X7 and 20X8 the balances were £30,000 and £26,000 again after writing off irrecoverable debts of £400 and £300 respectively.

Step 1   Calculate the allowances required at the end of each year:

   20X6   £24,000 × 4%   = £960

   20X7   £30,000 × 4%   = £1,200

   20X8   £26,000 × 4%   = £1,040

Step 2   Set up the allowance for doubtful debts at 31 December 20X6.

Allowance for doubtful debts adjustment account

Date 20X6	Details	£	Date 20X6	Details	£
31 Dec	Allowance for doubtful debts	960 960	31 Dec	Statement of profit or loss	960 960

Allowance for doubtful debts account

Date 20X6	Details	£	Date 20X6	Details	£
31 Dec			31 Dec	Allowance for doubtful debts adjustment	960
	Balance c/d	960	20X7		
			1 Jan	Balance b/d	960

The allowance has been set up by charging the whole amount to the allowance for doubtful debts adjustment account. This is then taken to the statement of profit or loss so no balance remains on that account. In contrast the allowance for doubtful debts is a statement of financial position account so it remains as the opening balance for 20X7.

Step 3   Increase allowance by (£1,200 – £960) = £240 to £1,200 at
          31 December 20X7.

Allowance for doubtful debts adjustment account

Date 20X7	Details	£	Date 20X7	Details	£
31 Dec	Allowance for doubtful debts	240 240	31 Dec	Statement of profit or loss	240 240

Allowance for doubtful debts account

Date	Details	£	Date	Details	£
20X6			20X6		
31 Dec	Balance c/d	960	31 Dec	Allowance for doubtful debts adjustment	960
20X7			20X7		
31 Dec	Balance c/d	1,200	1 Jan	Balance b/d	960
			31 Dec	Allowance for doubtful debts adjustment	240
		1,200			1,200
			20X8		
			1 Jan	Balance b/d	1,200

The allowance for doubtful debts adjustment account has only been charged with the amount that is necessary to bring the balance on the allowance up to this year's required amount of £1,200 – in this case £240.

> Step 4   Decrease allowance by (£1,200 – £1,040) = £160 to £1,040 as at 31 December 20X8.

Allowance for doubtful debts adjustment account

Date	Details	£	Date	Details	£
20X8			20X8		
31 Dec	Statement of profit or loss	160	31 Dec	Allowance for doubtful debts	160
		160			300

Allowance for doubtful debts account

Date	Details	£	Date	Details	£
20X6			20X6		
31 Dec	Balance c/d	960	31 Dec	Allowance for doubtful debts adjustment	960
20X7			20X7		
31 Dec	Balance c/d	1,200	1 Jan	Balance b/d	960
			31 Dec	Allowance for doubtful debts adjustment	240
		1,200			1,200
20X8			20X8		
31 Dec	Allowance for doubtful debts adjustment	160	1 Jan	Balance b/d	1,200
31 Dec	Balance c/d	1,040			
		1,200			1,200
			20X9		
			1 Jan	Balance b/d	1,040

In this case the allowance had to be reduced by £160 so the allowance for doubtful debts adjustment account was credited and the allowance account debited in order to bring the allowance account balance down to the amount required.

At each year end in the statement of financial position the receivables would appear as follows:

	20X6 £	20X7 £	20X8 £
Sales ledger control account	24,000	30,000	26,000
Less: allowance for doubtful debts	960	1,200	1,040
Receivables	23,040	28,800	24,960

Task 4

On 31 December 20X7 a business had a balance on its allowance for doubtful debts account of £1,500. At the year end of 31 December 20X8 its sales ledger control account balance was £60,000. On consideration of these debts it was decided that £2,400 were to be written off as irrecoverable debts and that an allowance of 1% was to be made against the remainder.

Prepare the journal entries, including narrative, to record the irrecoverable debt and the adjustment to the allowance.

Account name	Debit £	Credit £

Task 5

What is the double entry when the allowance for doubtful debts is to be **decreased**?

Account name	Debit £	Credit £
Allowance for doubtful debts (SFP)		
Allowance for doubtful debts adj (IS)		

Task 6

Setting up an allowance for doubtful debts is an example of which accounting concept?

Going concern/accruals/prudence/materiality/consistency.

CHAPTER OVERVIEW

- The accruals concept requires that sales on credit are recognised as soon as they are made rather than waiting until the cash is received from the customer – the prudence concept however requires that if money from a customer is unlikely to be received then it should not appear as an asset in the statement of financial position

- Any debts that are not going to be recovered should be written off as irrecoverable debts by debiting the irrecoverable debts expense account and crediting the sales ledger control account – the customer's individual account in the subsidiary sales ledger must also be credited with the amount of the irrecoverable debt

- If a customer eventually pays a debt that has already been written off as an irrecoverable debt then the bank / cash account is debited with the receipt and the irrecoverable debts expense account is credited

- A doubtful debt is one where there is concern about its recoverability – these are dealt with in the accounting records by setting up an allowance for doubtful debts

- In some cases the allowance will be against specific debts and in other cases a general allowance will be required at a percentage of the sales ledger control account balance less the specific allowance

- Once the allowance for doubtful debts has initially been set up then each year the balance must be increased or decreased to the amount that is required – this is done by debiting or crediting the allowance for doubtful debts adjustment account by the amount of the increase or decrease required

Keywords

Irrecoverable debt – a debt that it is believed will not be paid

Irrecoverable debts expense account – the expense account used to record the irrecoverable debts that are written off – the balance appears as an expense in the statement of profit or loss

Doubtful debts – amounts over which there is some doubt as to their recoverability

Allowance for doubtful debts – an amount that will be deducted from the sales ledger control account balance in the statement of financial position to reduce the balance for receivables to the prudent amount

Allowance for doubtful debts adjustment account – the account used to record the setting up and then adjustment of the allowance for doubtful debts – the balance appears initially as an expense in the statement of profit or loss), though in subsequent periods it may appear as income (when the allowance is reduced)

Specific allowance – an allowance against particular debts that are recognised as doubtful

General allowance – an allowance set up as a percentage of the receivables balance to reflect the fact that on average a certain percentage of debts will be doubtful

TEST YOUR LEARNING

Test 1

A business has receivables at 30 April 20XX of £25,673. Of these it was decided that two debts were never going to be recovered, £157 from H Taylor and £288 from C Phelps. These are to be written off as irrecoverable.

Write up the general ledger and sales ledger accounts necessary to record these irrecoverable debts.

General ledger

Sales ledger control account

	£		£

Irrecoverable debts expense account

	£		£

Sales ledger

H Taylor

	£		£

C Phelps

	£		£

Test 2

In 20X7 a business had written off an irrecoverable debt from a customer of £250. During 20X8 this amount was unexpectedly received from the customer.

Write up the general ledger accounts in full to reflect this receipt.

Bank account

	£		£

Irrecoverable debts expense account

	£		£

Test 3

At the end of the first year of trading a business has a sales ledger control account balance of £11,650. Of these it is decided that one debt of £350 is to be written off as irrecoverable. An allowance for doubtful debts is to be made against a further debt of £200 and a general allowance is required of 2% of the remainder.

(a) Calculate the amount of the allowance for doubtful debts that is required at the year end

£ ⬚

(b) Write up the irrecoverable debts expense account, sales ledger control account, allowance for doubtful debts adjustment account and allowance for doubtful debts account at the year end to reflect the position.

Irrecoverable debts expense account

	£		£

Sales ledger control account

	£		£

Allowance for doubtful debts adjustment account

	£		£

Allowance for doubtful debts account

	£		£

Test 4

On 1 January 20X7 there is a balance on a business's allowance for doubtful debts account of £1,460. At 31 December 20X7 the balance on the sales ledger control account is £42,570. Of this it is decided that £370 should be written off as an irrecoverable debt and an allowance for doubtful debts of 4% is required against the remainder.

At 31 December 20X8 the sales ledger control account total was £38,400 of which £400 is to be written off as an irrecoverable debt. An allowance for doubtful debts of 4% of the remainder is required.

Write up the irrecoverable debts expense account, the allowance for doubtful debts adjustment account and the allowance for doubtful debts account for 20X7 and 20X8.

Irrecoverable debts expense account

	£		£

Allowance for doubtful debts adjustment account

	£		£

Allowance for doubtful debts account

	£		£

chapter 9:
BANK RECONCILIATIONS

───────── **chapter coverage** 📖 ─────────

The cash book is one of the main books of prime entry and it is vital for any business to ensure control over its cash in hand and held at the bank. A key means of control is through the bank reconciliation process. The topics covered are:

✍ Purpose of bank reconciliations

✍ Checking the bank statement to the cash book

✍ Bank reconciliation statement

PURPOSE OF BANK RECONCILIATIONS

The bank reconciliation process, which is covered in detail for Level 2 in Control accounts, journals and the banking system involves checking transactions recorded in the bank account columns in the business's cash book to the bank statement issued by the business's bank.

In theory the balance on the cash book and on the bank statement should be the same, but in practice timing differences mean that they very rarely are.

Carrying out the bank reconciliation process has three purposes:

- To help **identify errors**:
    - made by the business in writing up its cash book
    - made by the bank in maintaining the business's bank account

- To help **identify omissions**:
    - from the cash book, such as bank charges and dishonoured cheques processed by the bank

    - from the bank statement, such as cheques that have been sent out to suppliers but have not yet been presented for payment

- To **verify the accuracy** of the balance for cash at bank as presented in financial statements at the end of the accounting period. Since the bank is a separate entity from the business, identifying and explaining the differences between the bank statement balance and the cash book balance means that a form of external verification has taken place.

CHECKING THE BANK STATEMENT TO THE CASH BOOK

When checking the bank statement to the cash book it should always be borne in mind that the bank statement and the cash book are mirror images of each other:

- A **debit entry in the cash book** – a receipt of money – will appear as a **credit on the bank statement**.

- A **credit entry in the cash book** – a payment of money – will appear as a **debit on the bank statement**.

A bank account which is 'in credit' according to the bank will have a debit balance on its cash book. A bank account which is 'overdrawn' according to the bank has a credit balance on the cash book – it is a liability, known as an overdraft, not an asset.

A bank statement for Anna Murphy is set out below as an example:

GREEN BANK

19 Market Square, Hentage, FR9 9PO

STATEMENT

Account Name:

Anna Murphy

Account No: 73-23-23 75487325

Date	Details	DEBITS (Payments)	CREDITS (Receipts)	Balance
		£	£	£
21/09	Balance b/d			10,000.00 CR
22/09	BGC		2,400.00	
	Bank charges	15.00		
	BACS – salaries	1,200.00		
	Cheque 134257	45.00		
	Standing order	50.00		
	Cheque returned unpaid	200.00		10,890.00 CR

When the bank statement for the period is received the following steps should be followed for comparison with the cash book:

Step 1   Work through all of the receipts shown on the bank statement comparing each one to entries in the Bank receipts column in the cash book. When each receipt has been agreed to the Bank receipts column the entry on the bank statement and in the cash book should be ticked.

Step 2   Work through all of the receipts shown on the bank statement comparing each one to entries in the Bank receipts column in the cash book. When each receipt has been agreed to the Bank receipts column the entry on the bank statement and in the cash book should be ticked.

Step 3   Any un-ticked items on the bank statement must be checked to ensure that the bank has not made a mistake.

Step 4   The un-ticked items on the bank statement can then be used to identify adjustments that are needed in the general ledger.

HOW IT WORKS

Anna Murphy has completed the process of checking her cash book to her bank statement. She is satisfied that the opening credit balance on the bank statement of £10,000 is correct but she has identified the following items that appear on the bank statement but do not appear in the cash book:

- A bank giro credit receipt from a customer with a customer code of SL876 for £2,400. She has discovered a remittance advice note from the customer which shows that £40 settlement discount was taken

- Bank charges of £15

- A BACS payment of net salaries of £1,200

- A cheque number 134257 paid for cash purchases (no VAT) of £45. In the bank payments column of the cash book a cheque with the same number appears with an amount of £54

- A standing order payment of £50. On checking with the bank Anna discovered that this was paid in error by the bank

- A cheque paid in for £200 from a customer with a customer code of SL452 has been dishonoured by the bank

It is possible that each of these points will require a journal entry to correct the general ledger accounts, and possibly also the memorandum sales and purchases ledgers.

Let us take each item in turn.

- **A bank giro credit receipt from a customer with a customer code of SL876 for £2,400. She has discovered a remittance advice note from the customer which shows that £40 settlement discount was taken**

Because a receipt by automated payment from a customer is not physically received as cash or a cheque by the business, it is very common for such items to appear on the bank statement before being entered in the cash book. Since this receipt and the discount taken have been validated by reference to the customer's remittance advice note, a journal to amend the cash book and other general ledger accounts can be prepared as follows:

Account name	Amount £	Debit (✓)	Credit (✓)
Bank	2,400	✓	
Sales ledger control	2,400		✓
Discounts allowed	40	✓	
Sales ledger control	40		✓

The sales ledger account SL876 also needs to be credited with £2,440 in total.

- **Bank charges of £15**

Bank charges are a cost to Anna's business so the journal entry needs to reflect this:

Account name	Amount £	Debit (✓)	Credit (✓)
Bank charges expense	15	✓	
Bank	15		✓

- **A BACS payment of net salaries of £1,200**

Payroll transactions are normally entered into the ledger accounts via the journal, so Anna needs to establish from the payroll exactly what entries should be made to record this payment in the general ledger. There is no doubt, however, that a payment by BACS (Bankers Automated Credit Service) should be credited to the bank payments column in the cash book.

- **A cheque number 134257 paid for £45. In the bank payments column of the cash book a cheque with the same number appears with an amount of £54**

Clearly the cheque should have been written in the cash book as £45 since this is the amount that the bank has paid out, so a journal entry needs to be made to correct the cash book and the purchases account. In the cash book £9 (£54 – £45) too much has been entered on the payments side, so the correcting journal is as follows:

Account name	Amount £	Debit (✓)	Credit (✓)
Bank	9	✓	
Purchases	9		✓

- **A standing order payment of £50. On checking with the bank Anna discovered that this was paid in error by the bank**

Although this payment has been made from Anna's bank account, reducing her balance by £50, it should not have been paid so it is up to the bank to process a correction. No correcting journal is needed for the ledger accounts.

- **A cheque paid in for £200 from a customer with a customer code of SL452 has been dishonoured by the bank**

When the cheque was entered in the cash book it would have been debited to bank and credited to sales ledger control. Now that the cheque has been dishonoured we must process a journal entry to remove the cash received and reinstate the debt:

Account name	Amount £	Debit (✓)	Credit (✓)
Sales ledger control	200	✓	
Bank	200		✓

The sales ledger account SL452 also needs to be debited with £200.

Task 1

The bank balance in D Ltd's cash book shows a debit balance of £12,450. The bank statement has the following items that do not appear in the cash book:

Standing order for rent of premises	400
BGC receipt from customer	230
Bank charges	25

Calculate the adjusted balance in D Ltd's cash book.

£ [   ]

Task 2

What is the journal entry for a cheque for £500 received from a customer and deposited with the bank but subsequently dishonoured?

Account name	Amount £	Debit (✓)	Credit (✓)

BANK RECONCILIATION STATEMENT

After correcting the cash book for all the legitimate items that appear on the bank statement we can calculate the correct balance for the bank account in the cash book. This does not mean however that the cash book balance will agree to that on the bank statement because we have not yet taken account of TIMING

DIFFERENCES, the inevitable time lag between recording receipts and payments in the cash book and their appearance on the bank statement.

- Cash and cheques paid in by the business are recorded in the cash book but the clearing system means there is a delay before they appear on the bank statement. Such amounts are known as OUTSTANDING LODGEMENTS.

- When cheques are written to suppliers they are entered in the cash book immediately. The cheques are then sent to the supplier, the supplier must take them to the bank and then there will be a clearing period before they appear on the bank statement. Those cheque payments that are in the cash book but not on the bank statement yet are known as UNPRESENTED CHEQUES.

HOW IT WORKS

Anna Murphy has processed all the journals prepared above and her three column cash book as at 22 September is as follows (we are ignoring the analysis columns):

Details	Cash receipts £	Bank receipts £	Disc allowed £	Details	Cheque number	Cash payments £	Bank payments £	Disc received £
Bal b/d	320.00	10,000.00		Supplier X	134255		700.00	
Customer A	400.00			Supplier Y	134256		480.00	
BGC		2,400.00	40.00	Bank charges			15.00	
Cash		720.00		BACS – salaries			1,200.00	
				Cash purchases	134257		45.00	
				Dishonoured cheque			200.00	
				Banking		720.00		
				Bal c/d			10,480.00	
	720.00	13,120.00	40.00			720.00	13,120.00	
Bal b/d		10,480.00						

We can now produce a BANK RECONCILIATION STATEMENT for Anna which will reconcile the corrected cash book balance for the bank account with the bank statement balance.

Firstly, we must remember to add back the standing order payment of £50 mistakenly made by the bank.

Next, by examining the Bank receipts column in the cash book we can see that there is an outstanding lodgement of cash and cheques for £720.00. This will increase the balance on the bank statement once they are recorded by the bank.

We can also see that there are two cheques which have not yet been paid out by the bank (cheque numbers 134255 and 134256). These are unpresented cheques which will make the bank statement figure smaller once they are paid. Therefore we deduct these in the bank reconciliation statement in order to come back to the cash book balance for the bank account of £10,480.00.

Bank reconciliation statement

	£	£
Balance per bank statement		10,890.00
Add back: standing order payment made in error		50.00
Add: outstanding lodgement		
Cash and cheques		720.00
Less: Unpresented cheques		
134255	700.00	
134256	480.00	
Total to subtract		(1,180.00)
Balance as per corrected cash book		10,480.00

Task 3

Which of the following will **not** appear in a bank reconciliation statement?

A Unpresented cheques

B Outstanding lodgements

C Journal entries

D Bank errors

CHAPTER OVERVIEW

- In order to check the accuracy of the bank columns in the cash book, it must be checked at regular intervals to the bank statements received

- The debit and credit entries and balances on the bank statement are the opposite to the entries in the ledger accounts as the bank is considering the accounting from its own perspective

- When checking the bank statement to the cash book, check each of the receipts and payments from the bank statement to the bank receipts and payments columns in the cash book and tick each agreed item in both the cash book and the bank statement

- Any un-ticked but valid items on the bank statement should be adjusted for in the general ledger (and the memorandum ledgers if necessary) by processing journal entries

- Once the relevant corrections have been made to the cash book it must be cast and balanced

- Any errors made by the bank which are highlighted must be adjusted by the bank and will also appear on the reconciliation

- The un-ticked items in the cash book are used to prepare the bank reconciliation statement

- The closing balance on the bank statement is reconciled to the corrected cash book balance in the bank reconciliation statement. The reconciling items will be bank errors, outstanding lodgements and unpresented cheques

Keywords

Outstanding lodgements – cheques that have been received and recorded in the cash receipts book but do not yet appear on the bank statement

Dishonoured cheque – cheque that is paid into a business's bank account and then is returned by the drawer's bank unpaid

Timing differences – the reason for the fact that the bank statement balance will rarely agree with the balance on the cash books, as receipts and payments recorded in the cash books will appear later in the bank statement due to the operation of the clearing system

Unpresented cheques – cheque payments that have been recorded in the cash payments book but do not yet appear on the bank statement

Bank reconciliation statement – a statement reconciling the bank statement balance to the corrected cash book balance

TEST YOUR LEARNING

Test 1

While comparing the cash book to the bank statement the following differences have appeared. Prepare journal entries for the general ledger accounts as appropriate for each of these items.

(a) A receipt from a credit customer has been recorded in the cash receipts book as £310.50 but appears correctly on the bank statement as £301.50

Account name	Amount £	Debit (✓)	Credit (✓)

(b) Bank charges on the bank statement are £15.80

Account name	Amount £	Debit (✓)	Credit (✓)

(c) A direct debit payment is in the bank statement to English Gas Co for £300.00 but has not been recorded in the cash payments book

Account name	Amount £	Debit (✓)	Credit (✓)

Test 2

Given below is a business's cash receipts and payments book for the week ending 8 March, the bank statement for that week and the bank reconciliation statement for the week ended 1 March.

You are required to prepare the bank reconciliation statement for the week ending 8 March.

Bank reconciliation as at 8 March

	£
Balance per bank statement	
Add:	
Total to add:	
Less:	
Total to subtract:	
Balance as per cash book	

Cash Receipts Book

Date	Details	£
4 March	J Killick	365.37
	D Francis	105.48
5 March	I Oliver	216.57
6 March	L Canter	104.78
7 March	R Trent	268.59
8 March	P Otter	441.78
		1,502.57

Cash Payments Book

Date	Details	Cheque number	£
4 March	L L Partners	002536	186.90
	P J Parler	002537	210.55
5 March	J K Properties	002538	500.00
	Harmer & Co	002539	104.78
	Plenith Ltd	002540	60.80
7 March	Wessex & Co	002541	389.40
8 March	Filmer Partners	002542	104.67
			1,557.10

Bank reconciliation statement at 1 March

	£	£
Balance per bank statement		835.68
Less: unpresented cheques		
002530	110.46	
002534	230.56	
002535	88.90	
		(429.92)
		405.76
Add: outstanding lodgement		102.45
Amended cash book balance		508.21

STATEMENT

first national
30 High Street
Benham
DR4 8TT

SOUTHFIELD ELECTRICAL LTD

Account number: 20-26-33 3126897

CHEQUE ACCOUNT

Sheet 023

Date		Paid out	Paid in	Balance
1 Mar	Balance b/f			835.68
4 Mar	Cheque no 002534	230.56		
	Credit		102.45	707.57
5 Mar	DD - National Telephones	145.00		
	Bank charges	7.80		554.77
6 Mar	Cheque No 002530	110.46		
	BACS - J T Turner		486.20	930.51
7 Mar	Credit		470.85	
	Cheque No 002537	210.55		
	Cheque No 002536	186.90		
	Cheque No 002538	500.00		503.91
8 Mar	Cheque No 002535	88.90		
	Credit		216.57	
	Cheque No 002539	104.78		526.80
8 Mar	Balance c/f			526.80

chapter 10:
CONTROL ACCOUNT RECONCILIATIONS

chapter coverage 📖

In this chapter we consider the reconciliations that are prepared for the sales ledger and purchases ledger control accounts with the sales and purchases ledgers, and the adjustments that may arise from the process. The topics covered are:

✍ Sales ledger control account and the sales ledger

✍ Purchases ledger control account and the purchases ledger

✍ Control accounts

✍ Control account reconciliations

✍ Sales ledger control account reconciliation

✍ Purchases ledger control account reconciliation

SALES LEDGER CONTROL ACCOUNT AND THE SALES LEDGER

Before we look at the control account procedures and reconciliations we will firstly run through how the accounting system works for sales on credit.

Accounting system for sales on credit

The process of accounting for sales on credit is as follows:

- The sales invoices sent to customers are recorded in the sales day book.

- The total of the sales day book is regularly posted to the sales ledger control account.

- The individual invoices in the sales day book are posted to the individual customers' accounts in the memorandum sales ledger.

- Receipts from credit customers are recorded in the cash receipts book.

- The total of the cash receipts book is regularly posted to the sales ledger control account.

- The individual receipts are posted to the individual customer's account in the sales ledger.

HOW IT WORKS

Fred Simpson has recently set up in business and is not registered for VAT. He currently has just three credit customers Bill, John and Karen. His sales day book, sales ledger control account and memorandum sales ledger accounts for the month of June are given below.

Sales day book

Date	Customer	Invoice no.	Ref	£
3/06	Bill	0045	SL01	235.00
5/06	Karen	0046	SL03	141.00
8/06	John	0047	SL02	176.25
15/06	Karen	0048	SL03	258.50
20/06	John	0049	SL02	117.50
28/06	Bill	0050	SL01	211.50
				1,139.75

These figures must be posted to the sales ledger control account and the individual customers' accounts in the sales ledger:

General ledger

Sales ledger control account

	£		£
Balance b/d	587.50		
SDB	1,139.75		

Sales ledger

Bill   SL01

Date	Details	£	Date	Details	£
1/06	Balance b/d	235.00			
3/06	SDB 0045	235.00			
28/06	SDB 0050	211.50			

John   SL02

Date	Details	£	Date	Details	£
1/06	Balance b/d	117.50			
8/06	SDB 0047	176.25			
20/06	SDB 0049	117.50			

Karen   SL03

Date	Details	£	Date	Details	£
1/06	Balance b/d	235.00			
5/06	SDB 0046	141.00			
15/06	SDB 0048	258.50			

The totals of the opening balances on each individual account in the memorandum ledger add up to the opening balance on the sales ledger control account.

Opening balances

	£
Bill	235.00
John	117.50
Karen	235.00
Sales ledger control account	587.50

This should always be the case if the accounting has been correctly carried out – the totals of the balances at any point in time on the individual accounts in the sales ledger should be equal to the balance on the sales ledger control account.

Now we will deal with the receipts from these customers in the month of June:

Cash receipts book

Date	Details	Ref	Bank £	Discounts allowed £	Sales ledger £
6/06	John	SL02	117.50		117.50
10/06	Bill	SL01	225.60	9.40	225.60
13/06	Karen	SL03	200.00		200.00
20/06	Bill	SL01	225.60	9.40	225.60
28/06	Karen	SL03	100.00		100.00
30/06	John	SL02	176.25		176.25
			1,044.95	18.80	1,044.95

These figures must also be posted to the general ledger and the sales ledger, and the accounts must be balanced.

General ledger

Sales ledger control account

	£		£
Balance b/d	587.50	CRB	1,044.95
SDB	1,139.75	CRB – discounts	18.80
	1,727.25	Balance c/d	663.50
			1,727.25
Balance b/d	663.50		

Sales ledger

Bill   SL01

Date	Details	£	Date	Details	£
1/06	Balance b/d	235.00	10/06	CRB	225.60
3/06	SDB 0045	235.00	10/06	CRB – discount	9.40
28/06	SDB 0050	211.50	20/06	CRB	225.60
			20/06	CRB – discount	9.40
				Balance c/d	211.50
		681.50			681.50
Balance b/d		211.50			

Date	Details	£	Date	Details	£
		John			**SL02**
1/06	Balance b/d	117.50	6/06	CRB	117.50
8/06	SDB 0047	176.25	30/06	CRB	176.25
20/06	SDB 0049	117.50	Balance c/d		117.50
		411.25			411.25
Balance b/d		117.50			

Date	Details	£	Date	Details	£
		Karen			**SL03**
1/06	Balance b/d	235.00	13/06	CRB	200.00
5/06	SDB 0046	141.00	28/06	CRB	100.00
15/06	SDB 0048	258.50	Balance c/d		334.50
		634.50			634.50
Balance b/d		334.50			

Closing balances

The total of each of the individual customer balances equals the balance on the sales ledger control account at the end of June:

	£
Bill	211.50
John	117.50
Karen	334.50
Sales ledger control balance	663.50

If the double entry has all been correctly carried out then the total of the list of sales ledger balances will always equal the balance on the sales ledger control account.

PURCHASES LEDGER CONTROL ACCOUNT AND THE PURCHASES LEDGER

Accounting for credit purchases

The accounting process for credit purchases and suppliers is precisely the same as for credit customers except that the entries in the accounts are the other way around.

- The purchase invoices received are recorded in the purchases day book.

- The total of the purchases day book is regularly posted to the purchases ledger control account.

- Individual invoices in the purchases day book are posted to the individual suppliers' accounts in the memorandum purchases ledger.

- Payments to credit suppliers are recorded in the cash payments book.

- The total of the cash payments book is regularly posted to the purchases ledger control account.

- Individual payments are posted to the individual suppliers' accounts in the purchases ledger.

Closing balances

In just the same way as with the accounting system for credit customers, if the double entry has been correctly performed then the closing balances on the individual supplier accounts in the purchases ledger should total back to the balance on the purchases ledger control account.

CONTROL ACCOUNTS

We will now look in more detail at the figures that are likely to appear in the sales ledger and purchases ledger control accounts as so far we have only considered the basic entries for invoices and cash.

Sales ledger control account

A typical sales ledger control account might have the following entries:

Sales ledger control account

	£		£
Balance b/d	X	Sales returns	X
Credit sales	X	Receipts from credit customers	X
Dishonoured cheques	X	Discounts allowed	X
		Irrecoverable debts written off	X
		Contra entry	X
		Balance c/d	X
	X		X
Balance b/d	X		

Balance b/d There is a debit opening balance on the account as the customers owe the business money. In some circumstances an individual customer may have a credit balance on their account in the sales ledger if they have overpaid, or are awaiting a credit note from the business for goods returned, but these would not show up separately on the control account.

Credit sales This is the figure that is posted from the sales day book.

Dishonoured cheques If a customer has paid for goods then there is a credit entry in the sales ledger control account but if the bank then returns the cheque as unpaid, ie the cheque has been 'dishonoured', the entry must be reversed by debiting the control account and crediting the bank account.

Sales returns This is the posting from the sales returns day book.

Receipts from credit customers This is the posting of the sales ledger column total from the cash receipts book.

Discounts allowed This is the posting from the memorandum discounts allowed column in the cash receipts book.

Irrecoverable debts written off This entry was covered in detail in Chapter 8.

Contra entry A CONTRA ENTRY, sometimes known as a set off, comes about where a customer of the business is also its supplier ie we both sell to them and buy from them on credit. The contra entry is an amount owing by the customer which is set off against the amount we owe to them as a supplier. This will be dealt with in more detail later in the chapter.

Balance c/d and b/d A debit balance is carried down on the credit side and brought down on the debit side.

Purchases ledger control account

A typical purchases ledger control account might look like this:

Purchases ledger control account

	£		£
		Balance b/d	X
Purchases returns	X	Credit purchases	X
Payments made to credit suppliers	X		
Discounts received	X		
Contra entry	X		
Balance c/d	X		
	X		X
		Balance b/d	X

Balance b/d The balance brought down will be on the credit side of the account as we owe the suppliers money.

Purchases returns This is the posting from the purchases returns day book.

Payments made to credit suppliers This is the posting from the cash payments book.

Discounts received This is the posting from the memorandum discounts received column total from the cash payments book.

Contra entry This is the other side of the posting from the sales ledger control account – see below for more detail.

Credit purchases This is the posting from the purchases day book.

Balance c/d and b/d A credit balance is carried down on the debit side and brought down on the credit side.

Contra entries

It is entirely possible that a person or business can be both a receivables (debtor) and a payable (creditor) of your business at the same time. This would come about if your business makes credit sales to this person and buys goods on credit from the same person. If the business is owed money by this person and also owes money to them then it would make sense to net the two amounts off against each other and only pay or receive the difference. This is what a CONTRA ENTRY reflects.

HOW IT WORKS

Dawn Fisher sells goods on credit to Emma Jones and currently Emma owes Dawn £210. Dawn also sometimes buys goods on credit from Emma and currently Dawn owes Emma £100. The accounts for Emma in Dawn's sales ledger and purchases ledger appear as follows:

Sales ledger

Emma Jones			
	£		£
Balance b/d	210		

Purchases ledger

Emma Jones			
	£		£
		Balance b/d	100

Dawn and Emma have discussed this situation and have agreed that rather than Emma paying Dawn £210 and then Dawn paying Emma £100 it would be easier to net the two amounts off and for Emma simply to pay Dawn the remaining £110 that she owes.

This £100 will be debited to Emma's account in the purchases ledger and credited to her account in the sales ledger.

Sales ledger

Emma Jones			
	£		£
Balance b/d	210	Contra	100
		Balance c/d	110
	210		210
Balance b/d	110		

Purchases ledger

Emma Jones

	£		£
Contra	100	Balance b/d	100

This leaves Dawn with a balance of £110 on Emma's account in the sales ledger reflecting the agreed situation.

However if entries are made in the memorandum ledgers then they must also be reflected in the general ledger by a journal entry:

Account name	Amount £	Debit (✓)	Credit (✓)
Purchases ledger control	100	✓	
Sales ledger control	100		✓

General ledger

Sales ledger control account

	£		£
		Contra	100

Purchases ledger control account

	£		£
Contra	100		

Task 1

A business owes £500 to a supplier and that supplier also owes the business £800. They agree to net these amounts off.

Prepare the journal entry to reflect this agreement in the general ledger.

Account name	Debit £	Credit £

CONTROL ACCOUNT RECONCILIATIONS

We have seen that if all of the double entry in the general ledger and entries in the memorandum ledger are correctly carried out then the totals of the balances on the memorandum ledger should be equal to the balance on the control account.

Control account balances

The balances on the sales ledger and purchases ledger control accounts are the figures that will appear in the trial balance for receivables and payables and eventually in the financial statements. Therefore it is important to ensure that these figures are correct. This is done by carrying out a SALES LEDGER CONTROL ACCOUNT RECONCILIATION and a PURCHASES LEDGER CONTROL ACCOUNT RECONCILIATION.

The process involves comparing the balance on the control account to the total of the balances of the individual accounts in the memorandum ledger. If the two totals do not agree then there have been errors made in either the control account or the memorandum ledger or both. These errors must be investigated, discovered and corrected.

Some of the errors might have been made in the double entry in the general ledger so they affect the control account. Other errors might have been made when posting entries to the individual accounts in the memorandum ledger or in listing the balances in the memorandum ledger.

To summarise, the purpose of these reconciliations is to help:

- **Identify errors**
- **Identify omissions**

Errors affecting the control account

Typical types of errors that may have been made in the double entry in the general ledger, therefore affecting the control account balance may include the following:

- The books of prime entry may have been undercast or overcast so the incorrect total is posted to the control account (this would not affect the individual balances since these are posted with individual transactions from the books of prime entry).

- Postings from the books of prime entry may have been made to the wrong side of the control account.

- The discounts recorded in the cash book may be incorrectly treated in the control account.

- An irrecoverable debt may not have been entered into the general ledger although it was written off in the sales ledger.

- A contra entry may have been made in the memorandum ledgers but not entered into the general ledger accounts.

Errors affecting the list of balances

Some errors will not affect the double entry in the general ledger but will mean that the individual balances in the memorandum ledger are not correct or that these balances are listed and totalled incorrectly. Typical errors include the following:

- A transaction from the books of prime entry might be posted to the wrong account in the memorandum ledger.

- Entries from the books of prime entry may be posted to the wrong side of the memorandum ledger account.

- An entry from the books of prime entry may be posted as the wrong amount to the memorandum ledger account.

- A balance on an account in the memorandum ledger may be included in the list of balances as the wrong amount or as the wrong type of balance, eg a debit rather than a credit.

Task 2

If the sales day book total for a week is overcast by £1,000 this would affect the sales ledger control account/the individual accounts in the sales ledger.

SALES LEDGER CONTROL ACCOUNT RECONCILIATION

A sales ledger control account reconciliation is a comparison of the balance on the sales ledger control account to the total of the list of balances from the sales ledger to check for errors and omissions. This is carried out on a regular basis, usually monthly.

HOW IT WORKS

Dawn Fisher is carrying out her sales ledger control account reconciliation at the end of December 20X4. The balance on the sales ledger control account is £11,578. The total of the list of account balances from the sales ledger is £11,104.

Step 1   Check whether the control account total agrees to the total of the memorandum ledger balances.

	£
Control account total	11,578
List of balances	11,104
Difference	474

The reasons for this difference must be investigated.

Step 2   The control account and the individual accounts and balances must be checked and any errors or omissions noted.

In Dawn's case the following errors were noted:

(a)   A page of the cash receipts book had been undercast by £100

(b)   The total from the sales day book for a week had been posted as £2,340 instead of £2,430

(c)   An irrecoverable debt of £80 had been written off in the individual customer's account but not in the general ledger

(d)   An invoice to G Harper for £250 had been entered into the account of G Draper instead

(e)   A cash receipt from David Carr had been entered into his account as £175 instead of the correct figure from the cash receipts book of £157

(f)   A debit balance of £406 on one customer's account had been omitted from the list of balances

(g)   A credit balance of £20 on a customer's account had been included in the list of balances as a debit balance

Step 3   The accounts must be adjusted for any errors that affect them. We shall take each one in turn and identify the adjustment needed:

(a)   **A page of the cash receipts book had been undercast by £100**

The total from the cash receipts book would have been credited to the sales ledger control account so if it was undercast by £100 the account must be credited with a further £100

Adjustment	Amount	Debit (✓)	Credit (✓)
	£		
Sales ledger control	100		✓

(b) **The total from the sales day book for a week had been posted as £2,340 instead of £2,430**

The total from the sales day book is debited to the sales ledger control account and as the entry was for £90 too little an extra debit entry of £90 is required

Adjustment	Amount £	Debit (✓)	Credit (✓)
Sales ledger control	90	✓	

(c) **An irrecoverable debt of £80 had been written off in the individual customer's account but not in the general ledger**

To write off an irrecoverable debt the sales ledger control account must be credited

Adjustment	Amount £	Debit (✓)	Credit (✓)
Sales ledger control	80		✓

(d) **An invoice to G Harper for £250 had been entered into the account of G Draper instead**

This does not affect the sales ledger control account at all and also does not affect the total of the sales ledger balances – the correct amount was entered on the correct side, but in the wrong account

(e) **A cash receipt from David Carr had been entered into his account as £175 instead of the correct figure from the cash receipts book of £157**

The receipt was recorded at a figure of £18 too much therefore the balance on this customer's account should be £18 higher

Adjustment	Amount £	Debit (✓)	Credit (✓)
Sales ledger balances	18	✓	

(f) **A debit balance of £406 on one customer's account had been omitted from the list of balances**

The balance omitted must be added in to the total of the list of balances.

Adjustment	Amount £	Debit (✓)	Credit (✓)
Sales ledger balances	406	✓	

(g) **A credit balance of £20 on a customer's account had been included in the list of balances as a debit balance**

The error must be removed by removing the £20 debit balance, and then the correct credit balance of £20 must be entered, so in the end the correction is a £40 credit in the list of balances

Adjustment	Amount £	Debit (✓)	Credit (✓)
Sales ledger balances	40		✓

Step 4   Process the adjustments to the sales ledger control account.

Sales ledger control account

	£		£
Balance b/d	11,578	(a) Cash receipts books	100
(b) Sales day book	90	(c) Irrecoverable debt	80
		Balance c/d	11,488
	11,668		11,668
Balance b/d	11,488		

Step 5   Adjust the total of the list of balances by adding or deducting the errors that affect this total.

	£
Original total	11,104
Add: (e) cash receipt adjustment (175 – 157)	18
Add: (f) balance omitted	406
Less:(g) credit balance included as debit balance	(40)
Amended total of the list of balances	11,488

The amended total of the list of balances now agrees to the amended sales ledger control account balance, and the general ledger and sales ledger are reconciled. The balance on the sales ledger control account can now be used as the receivables figure in the trial balance.

Task 3

The total of the discounts allowed column from the cash receipts book of £120 was not posted for a period. Set out the adjustment necessary in the sales ledger control account.

Adjustment	Amount £	Debit (✓)	Credit (✓)

PURCHASES LEDGER CONTROL ACCOUNT RECONCILIATION

A purchases ledger control account reconciliation works in exactly the same manner as a sales ledger control account reconciliation with the entries on the opposite sides, and no entry possible for irrecoverable debts.

HOW IT WORKS

Dawn Fisher is currently preparing her purchases ledger control account reconciliation at the end of October 20X4. The balance on the purchases ledger control account was £9,240 and the total of the list of balances from the purchases ledger was £9,040.

The following errors and omissions were noted:

(a) One page of the purchases day book has been undercast by £100

(b) An invoice has been posted to an individual account in the purchases ledger as £863 instead of the correct figure from the purchases day book of £683

(c) The total of discounts received of £160 was credited to the purchases ledger control account

(d) One of the balances in the purchases ledger was included in the total at a figure of £235 instead of £325

(e) A contra entry for £70 had been made in the purchases ledger but not in the general ledger

Step 1   The accounts must be adjusted for any errors that affect them. We shall take each one in turn and identify the adjustment needed:

(a) **One page of the purchases day book has been undercast by £100**

The total from the purchases day book is credited to the purchases ledger control account and therefore if it was undercast by £100 then the account must be credited with £100

Adjustment	Amount £	Debit (✓)	Credit (✓)
Purchases ledger control	100		✓

(b) **An invoice has been posted to an individual account in the purchases ledger as £863 instead of the correct figure from the purchases day book of £683**

An invoice would be posted to the credit side of the supplier's account – in this case it was posted at a figure £180 too high and therefore the balances would be reduced when the account was amended

Adjustment	Amount £	Debit (✓)	Credit (✓)
Purchases ledger balances	180	✓	

(c) **The total of discounts received of £160 was credited to the purchases ledger control account**

The discounts received should have been debited to the purchases ledger control account – instead they were credited and therefore not only should there be one debit of £160 but two, one to cancel out the credit and one to put the debit entry in, therefore a debit of £320

Adjustment	Amount £	Debit (✓)	Credit (✓)
Purchases ledger control	320	✓	

(d) **One of the balances in the purchases ledger was included in the total at a figure of £235 instead of £325**

The balance that was misstated was shown as £90 too small – therefore the balances need to be increased by £90

Adjustment	Amount £	Debit (✓)	Credit (✓)
Purchases ledger balances	90		✓

(e) **A contra entry for £70 had been made in the purchases ledger but not in the general ledger**

The contra entry must be put into the purchases ledger control account as a debit of £70

Adjustment	Amount £	Debit (✓)	Credit (✓)
Purchases ledger control	70	✓	

Step 2 Adjust the control account balance for the errors that affect it.

Purchases ledger control account

	£		£
		Balance b/d	9,240
(c) Discounts	320	(a) Purchases day book	100
(e) Contra	70		
Balance c/d	8,950		
	9,340		9,340
		Balance b/d	8,950

Step 3 Adjust the total of the list of balances for any errors that affect the individual balances or their total.

	£
Original total	9,040
Less: (b) invoice misposting (863 − 683)	(180)
Add: (e) balance misstated	90
	8,950

Now the amended balance on the purchases ledger control account of £8,950 agrees with the amended list of balances in the purchases ledger. This figure of £8,950 can now be used as the payables figure in the trial balance.

Task 4

An invoice for £350 was entered into the individual supplier's account in the purchases ledger on the wrong side of the account. How should this be adjusted for in the purchases ledger control account reconciliation?

Adjustment	Amount £	Debit (✓)	Credit (✓)

Task 5

Which of the following items will appear as an item posted to the purchases ledger control account?

A   Irrecoverable debts written off

B   Returns inwards of the period

C   Discounts allowed in total in the period

D   Discounts received in total in the period

Task 6

A business maintains a sales ledger control account. A debt of £1,500 is to be written off. Which of the following entries is correct (ignore VAT)?

A   Debit personal account of the customer, credit irrecoverable debts expense

B   Debit irrecoverable debts expense, credit sales ledger control

C   Debit sales ledger control, credit irrecoverable debt expense

D   Debit irrecoverable debts expense, credit personal account of the customer

CHAPTER OVERVIEW

- The sales ledger control account is debited with the sales invoices from the sales day book and credited with cash receipts and discounts from the cash receipts book

- The individual accounts for each customer in the sales ledger are also debited with each invoice total and credited with the cash and discounts

- If all of the entries are correctly carried out then the total of the closing balances on the individual accounts from the sales ledger should agree to the balance on the sales ledger control account

- The same system applies to accounting for credit suppliers although the entries are all on the opposite sides

- The sales ledger control account will potentially have entries for sales returns, dishonoured cheques, irrecoverable debts written off and contra entries as well as the basic entries for invoices, cash and discounts

- The purchases ledger control account will potentially have entries for purchases returns and a contra entry as well as the basic entries for invoices, cash and discounts

- A contra entry is caused by netting off a sales ledger and a purchases ledger balance with the same party – in the general ledger this is done by debiting the purchases ledger control account and crediting the sales ledger control account – in the memorandum ledgers the customer's account will be credited and the supplier's account debited

- If all of the entries in the general ledger and memorandum ledger have not been properly performed then the ledger balances total will not agree to the balance on the control account – in which case the errors that cause the difference must be discovered and adjusted

- When a control account reconciliation has been completed and adjustments have been made, the control account balance and the total of the list of balances should agree

Keywords

Contra entry – an amount owed by a customer which is set off against an amount owed to them as a supplier

Sales ledger control account reconciliation – an exercise which agrees the balance on the sales ledger control account to the total of the list of balances in the sales ledger

Purchases ledger control account reconciliation – an exercise which agrees the balance on the purchases ledger control account to the total of the list of balances in the purchases ledger

TEST YOUR LEARNING

Test 1

The balance on a business's sales ledger control account at the end of June was £41,774 and the total of the list of balances from the sales ledger came to £41,586.

The following errors were discovered:

(a) The sales day book was undercast by £100 on one page.

(b) A page from the sales returns day book with a total of £450 had not been posted to the control account although the individual returns had been recorded in the memorandum ledger.

(c) An invoice from the sales day book had been posted to the individual account of the customer as £769 instead of the correct figure of £679.

(d) A discount allowed to one customer of £16 had been posted to the wrong side of the customer's account in the sales ledger.

(e) An irrecoverable debt of £210 had been written off in the account in the sales ledger but not in the general ledger.

(f) A credit balance in the memorandum ledger of £125 had been included in the list of balances as a debit balance.

Use the following table to show the THREE adjustments you need to make to the sales ledger control account.

Adjustment	Amount £	Debit (✓)	Credit (✓)

Test 2

The balance on a business's purchases ledger control account at the end of June is £38,694 and the total of the list of balances in the memorandum purchases ledger came to £39,741.

The following errors were noted for the month:

(a) A page in the purchases returns day book was overcast by £300.

(b) A total from the cash payments book of £3,145 was posted in the general ledger as £3,415.

(c) Settlement discounts received from suppliers of £267 were omitted from both the general ledger and the purchases ledger.

(d) A credit note from a supplier for £210 was entered into the supplier's account in the purchases ledger as £120.

(e) A debit balance on an account in the purchases ledger of £187 was omitted from the list of balances.

(f) A credit balance in the purchases ledger should have been included in the list as £570 but instead was recorded as £770.

Use the following table to show the THREE adjustments you need to make to the purchases ledger control account.

Adjustment	Amount £	Debit (✓)	Credit (✓)

chapter 11:
THE TRIAL BALANCE, ERRORS AND THE SUSPENSE ACCOUNT

chapter coverage 📖

So far in this Text we have seen how to account for non-current assets and adjustments such as depreciation, accruals and prepayments, irrecoverable and doubtful debts and inventory. We have also looked at various reconciliations that are prepared at the end of an accounting period and how the errors that these identify can be adjusted. In Processing bookkeeping transactions we saw how to extract an initial trial balance and also how to redraft it if necessary. We now move on to look at how to complete a trial balance when taking into account the various adjustments that we have encountered.

In this chapter we first briefly revise the types of error that are found in ledger accounts, and whether they cause a suspense account on the trial balance or not. We then work through an example showing how to go from the year end balances for a sole trader to the completed trial balance via an initial trial balance and various accounting adjustments. In doing so we cover accounting for errors using the suspense account. The topics covered are:

✎ Types of error

✎ Completing the trial balance

TYPES OF ERROR

In any accounting system there are several types of error that can be made when making entries to the ledger accounts. Some of these will be identified when reconciliations are prepared, as we saw in Chapters 9 and 10, and some will come to light when a trial balance is extracted. There are also, however, a number of types of error that do not affect the balancing of the trial balance – despite the error, the trial balance will still balance.

Errors leading to an imbalance on the trial balance

The following types of error will mean that the debit balances on the trial balance do not equal the credit balances, so a suspense account must be opened and cleared.

Type of error	Description	Correction	Example
One-sided entry	Only one side of the double entry has been made in the ledger accounts, eg the debit and not the credit	Make the missing entry and post the other side to the suspense account	*Error* £10 cash purchase only credited to cash *Correction* Debit Purchases £10 Credit Suspense £10
Entry duplicated on one side, nothing on the other	Instead of posting a transaction as a debit in one account and a credit in another, both accounts are posted with debit entries, or both with credit entries. One account is correct but the other is out of balance by twice the amount of the posting	Post the account that was posted on the wrong side with twice the amount, and post the other side to suspense	*Error* £10 cash purchase credited to both cash and purchases *Correction* Debit Purchases £20 Credit Suspense £20

Type of error	Description	Correction	Example
Unequal entries, normally caused by a transposition error	The correct amount is entered on one side, but there is an error in writing in the other side of the entry. Often this is caused by a transposition error in the incorrect entry, where the digits in a number are transposed (swapped round). If this is the only error in the accounts then the difference between the debits and the credits will be divisible by 9	In the account with the wrong posting, post an amount to bring the entry to the right amount, and post the other side to suspense	*Error* £10 cash purchase debited to purchases as £100 (correct credit to cash) *Correction* Debit Suspense £90 Credit Purchases £90
Account balance incorrectly transferred to the trial balance	This may be because of a calculation error when calculating the balance on a ledger account, or it may be that a balance which has been calculated correctly in the ledger is entered incorrectly to the trial balance	In the account with the wrong balance, post an amount to bring the balance to the right amount, and post the other side to suspense	*Error* £1,000 debit balance on purchases account written into trial balance as a £100 debit balance *Correction* Debit Purchases £900 Credit Suspense £900

Type of error	Description	Correction	Example
Balance omission	A balance on a general ledger account is omitted from the trial balance completely	Enter the missing balance on the correct side and enter the suspense account with the same amount on the other side	*Error* £1,000 debit balance on purchases account omitted *Correction* Debit Purchases on trial balance £1,000 Credit Suspense on trial balance £1,000

Errors not revealed by an imbalance on the trial balance

Unfortunately, there are also some types of error that do not cause a difference on the trial balance and therefore cannot be revealed through the trial balance process – though they must still be found of course!

Type of error	Description	Correction	Example
Error of principle	The double entry is arithmetically correct but the wrong type of account has been used eg a non-current asset account is debited with expenses	Remove the incorrect entry and post it to the correct account	*Error* Motor expenses of £100 have been debited to the motor vehicles cost account *Correction* Debit Motor expenses £100 Credit Motor vehicles cost £100

Type of error	Description	Correction	Example
Error of original entry	Both the debit and the credit entries have been made using the wrong amount because: – the transaction was recorded in the book of prime entry at the incorrect amount, or – the wrong figure was picked up from the primary record (eg a transposition error was made), this incorrect figure was used to write up the book of prime entry and so to make both the debit and the credit entry	In both accounts, post an amount to bring the entry to the right amount	*Error* Motor expenses of £100 have been recorded as £10 in the purchases day book *Correction* Debit Motor expenses £90 Credit Purchases ledger control £90
Error of omission	A transaction is completely omitted from the ledger accounts	Make the appropriate posting	*Error* Cash purchases of £10 have not been recorded *Correction* Debit Purchases £10 Credit Cash £10

Type of error	Description	Correction	Example
Reversal of entries	The correct figure has been used and a debit and a credit entry made but the debit and the credit are on the wrong side of the respective accounts	Remove the incorrect entries and make the correct ones by posting the accounts correctly but with double the amount	*Error* Cash purchases of £10 have been debited to cash and credited to purchases *Correction* Debit Purchases £20 Credit Cash £20
Error of commission	The double entry is arithmetically correct but a wrong account of the same type has been used eg a phone expense is debited to the electricity account rather than the phone account	Remove the incorrect entry and post it to the correct account	*Error* Motor expenses of £100 have been debited to the office expenses account *Correction* Debit Motor expenses £100 Credit Office expenses £100

COMPLETING THE TRIAL BALANCE

We will now work through a comprehensive example which will take you from ledger account balances through to a completed trial balance via adjustments and a suspense account.

HOW IT WORKS

Given below are the brought down balances on the ledger accounts at the end of the day on 31 March 20X4, the year end, for John Thompson, who is not registered for VAT.

Building at cost

			£			£
31 Mar	Balance b/d		100,000			

Furniture and fittings at cost

			£			£
31 Mar	Balance b/d		4,800			

Motor vehicles at cost

			£			£
31 Mar	Balance b/d		32,700			

Computer at cost

			£			£
31 Mar	Balance b/d		2,850			

Accumulated depreciation – building

	£				£
		31 Mar	Balance b/d		4,000

Accumulated depreciation – furniture and fittings

	£				£
		31 Mar	Balance b/d		1,920

Accumulated depreciation – motor vehicles

	£				£
		31 Mar	Balance b/d		7,850

Accumulated depreciation – computer

	£				£
		31 Mar	Balance b/d		950

Inventory

			£			£
31 Mar	Balance b/d		4,400			

Bank/cash

			£			£
31 Mar	Balance b/d		3,960			

Petty cash

			£			£
31 Mar	Balance b/d		100			

Sales ledger control

		£			£
31 Mar	Balance b/d	15,240			

Purchases ledger control

		£			£
			31 Mar	Balance b/d	5,010

Capital

		£			£
			31 Mar	Balance b/d	130,000

Sales revenue

		£			£
			31 Mar	Balance b/d	155,020

Sales returns

		£			£
31 Mar	Balance b/d	2,100			

Purchases

		£			£
31 Mar	Balance b/d	80,200			

Purchases returns

		£			£
			31 Mar	Balance b/d	1,400

Bank charges

		£			£
31 Mar	Balance b/d	200			

Discounts allowed

		£			£
31 Mar	Balance b/d	890			

Discounts received

		£			£
			31 Mar	Balance b/d	1,260

Wages

		£			£
31 Mar	Balance b/d	32,780			

Rates

		£			£
31 Mar	Balance b/d	5,500			

Telephone

		£			£
31 Mar	Balance b/d	1,140			

Electricity

		£			£
31 Mar	Balance b/d	1,480			

Insurance

		£			£
31 Mar	Balance b/d	1,500			

Motor expenses

		£			£
31 Mar	Balance b/d	1,580			

Office expenses

		£			£
31 Mar	Balance b/d	960			

Allowance for doubtful debts

		£			£
			31 Mar	Balance b/d	220

Loan

		£			£
			31 Mar	Balance b/d	820

Drawings

		£			£
31 Mar	Balance b/d	15,800			

The first stage is to transfer all of the closing balances on the ledger accounts to the trial balance, add it up and check that it balances. If it does not balance, first check your additions and if this doesn't clear it, then open up a suspense account to make the debits and credits equal.

Draft trial balance as at 31 March 20X4

	Debit £	Credit £
Buildings at cost	100,000	
Furniture and fittings at cost	4,800	
Motor vehicles at cost	32,700	
Computer at cost	2,850	
Accumulated depreciation – buildings		4,000
Accumulated depreciation – furniture and fittings		1,920
Accumulated depreciation – motor vehicles		7,850
Accumulated depreciation – computer		950
Inventory	4,400	
Bank/cash	3,960	
Petty cash	100	
Sales ledger control	15,240	
Purchases ledger control		5,010
Capital		130,000
Sales revenue		155,020
Sales returns	2,100	
Purchases	80,200	
Purchases returns		1,400
Bank charges	200	
Discounts allowed	890	
Discounts received		1,260
Wages	32,780	
Rates	5,500	
Telephone	1,140	
Electricity	1,480	
Insurance	1,500	
Motor expenses	1,580	
Office expenses	960	
Allowance for doubtful debts		220
Loan		820
Drawings	15,800	
Suspense	270	
	308,450	308,450

Suspense account

In this case the credit total was £270 larger than the debit total and so a suspense account was opened for the difference. The suspense account must of course be cleared and the errors that were discovered are given below:

(a) The purchases returns account was overcast by £100.

(b) £200 of office expenses has been charged to the motor expenses account.

(c) Discounts allowed of £170 have been correctly accounted for in the sales ledger control account but omitted from the discounts allowed account.

We must now prepare journal entries to correct these errors and to clear the suspense account.

Journal entries

(a) As purchase returns are a credit balance if the account has been overstated then the purchases returns account must be debited and the suspense account credited.

Account name	Amount £	Debit (✓)	Credit (✓)
Purchases returns	100	✓	
Suspense	100		✓

(b) The motor expenses account has been wrongly debited with office expenses so the motor expenses account must be credited and office expenses debited.

Account name	Amount £	Debit (✓)	Credit (✓)
Office expenses	200	✓	
Motor expenses	200		✓

(c) The correct double entry for discounts allowed is a debit to the discounts allowed account and a credit to sales ledger control. The credit has been done but the debit is missing. Therefore we must debit discounts allowed and credit the suspense account.

Account name	Amount £	Debit (✓)	Credit (✓)
Discounts allowed	170	✓	
Suspense	170		✓

Year end adjustments

You are also given information about the following year end adjustments that must be made:

(a) Depreciation is to be charged for the year using the following depreciation policy:

- Building – 2% straight line
- Furniture and fittings – 20% straight line
- Motor vehicles – 30% reducing balance
- Computer – 33⅓ % straight line

(b) Rates of £500 are to be accrued

(c) The insurance account includes an amount of £300 that relates to the year ended 31 March 20X5

(d) An irrecoverable debt of £240 is to be written off

(e) An allowance for 2% of the remaining debts is required

We must now prepare the journal entries that will complete these adjustments and close off the accounts for the period.

Journal entries

(a) The accumulated depreciation accounts in the trial balance are as at the beginning of the year since the annual depreciation charge has yet to be accounted for. In each case the double entry is to debit a depreciation charge account and to credit the relevant accumulated depreciation account.

	Debit £	Credit £
Depreciation charge – building (100,000 × 2%)	2,000	
Accumulated depreciation – building		2,000
Depreciation charge – furniture and fittings (4,800 × 20%)	960	
Accumulated depreciation – furniture and fittings		960
Depreciation charge – motor vehicles ((32,700 – 7,850) × 30%)	7,455	
Accumulated depreciation – motor vehicles		7,455
Depreciation charge – computer (2,850 × 33⅓)	950	
Accumulated depreciation – computer		950

(b) Rates of £500 are to be accrued.

	Debit £	Credit £
Rates	500	
Accruals		500

(c) Insurance has been prepaid by £300

	Debit £	Credit £
Prepayments	300	
Insurance		300

(d) An irrecoverable debt of £240 is to be written off

	Debit £	Credit £
Irrecoverable debts expense	240	
Sales ledger control		240

(e) An allowance for doubtful debts of 2% of the remaining debts is required.

	£
Allowance required = (15,240 – 240) × 2%	300
Current level of allowance	220
Increase in allowance	80

	Debit £	Credit £
Allowance for doubtful debts adjustment	80	
Allowance for doubtful debts		80

Closing inventory

The closing inventory has been counted and valued at £5,200.

The inventory figure in the draft trial balance is the opening inventory which will eventually be debited to the statement of profit or loss as part of cost of sales. The closing inventory must now be entered into the accounts with a journal entry.

	Debit £	Credit £
Inventory – statement of financial position	5,200	
Inventory – statement of profit or loss		5,200

Updating ledger accounts

All the journal entries have now been made for the correction of errors, adjustments and closing inventory. These journals must now be entered into the ledger accounts and the ledger accounts balanced to give their amended closing balances. This means that a number of new ledger accounts have to be opened.

Errors

(a)

Purchases returns

		£			£
31 March	Journal	100	31 March	Balance b/d	1,400
31 March	Balance c/d	1,300			
		1,400			1,400
			31 March	Balance b/d	1,300

Suspense account

		£			£
31 March	Balance b/d	270	31 March	Journal	100

(b)

Office expenses

		£			£
31 March	Balance b/d	960			
31 March	Journal	200	31 March	Balance c/d	1,160
		1,160			1,160
31 March	Balance b/d	1,160			

Motor expenses

		£			£
31 March	Balance b/d	1,580	31 March	Journal	200
			31 March	Balance c/d	1,380
		1,580			1,580
31 March	Balance b/d	1,380			

(c)

Discounts allowed

		£			£
31 March	Balance b/d	890			
31 March	Journal	170	31 March	Balance c/d	1,060
		1,060			1,060
31 March	Balance b/d	1,060			

Suspense account

		£			£
31 March	Balance b/d	270	31 March	Journal	100
			31 March	Journal	170
		270			270

Year end adjustments

(a) Depreciation charges for the year

Depreciation charge – building

		£		£
31 March	Journal	2,000		

Accumulated depreciation – building

		£			£
			31 March	Balance b/d	4,000
31 March	Balance c/d	6,000	31 March	Journal	2,000
		6,000			6,000
			31 March	Balance b/d	6,000

Depreciation charge – furniture and fittings

		£		£
31 March	Journal	960		

Accumulated depreciation – furniture and fittings

		£			£
			31 March	Balance b/d	1,920
31 March	Balance c/d	2,880	31 March	Journal	960
		2,880			2,880
			31 March	Balance b/d	2,880

Depreciation charge – motor vehicles

		£		£
31 March	Journal	7,455		

Accumulated depreciation – motor vehicles

		£			£
			31 March	Balance b/d	7,850
31 March	Balance c/d	15,305	31 March	Journal	7,455
		15,305			15,305
			31 March	Balance b/d	15,305

Depreciation charge – computer

		£		£
31 March	Journal	950		

BPP
LEARNING MEDIA

Accumulated depreciation – computer

		£			£
			31 March	Balance b/d	950
31 March	Balance c/d	1,900	31 March	Journal	950
		1,900			1,900
			31 March	Balance b/d	1,900

(b) Rates accrual

Rates

		£			£
31 March	Balance b/d	5,500			
31 March	Journal	500	31 March	Balance c/d	6,000
		6,000			6,000
31 March	Balance b/d	6,000			

Accruals

		£			£
			31 March	Journal	500

(c) Insurance prepaid

Insurance

		£			£
31 March	Balance b/d	1,500	31 March	Journal	300
			31 March	Balance c/d	1,200
		1,500			1,500
31 March	Balance b/d	1,200			

Prepayments

		£		£
31 March	Journal	300		

(d) Irrecoverable debt write off

Irrecoverable debts expense

		£		£
31 March	Journal	240		

Sales ledger control

		£			£
31 March	Balance b/d	15,240	31 March	Journal	240
			31 March	Balance c/d	15,000
		15,240			15,240
31 March	Balance b/d	15,000			

(e) Allowance for doubtful debts

Allowance for doubtful debts adjustment

		£		£
31 March	Journal	80		

Allowance for doubtful debts

		£			£
			31 March	Balance b/d	220
31 March	Balance c/d	300	31 March	Journal	80
		300			300
			31 March	Balance b/d	300

Closing inventory

Inventory – statement of financial position

	£		£
31 March Journal	5,200		

Inventory – statement of profit or loss

	£			£
		31 March	Journal	5,200

Once all the ledger accounts have been updated for the journal entries a new final trial balance is drawn up which reflects all of the error corrections and adjustments.

Note that we now have three inventory account balances. Do not worry about this at the moment as it will be explained in Chapter 12.

Final trial balance as at 31 March 20X4

	Debit £	Credit £
Buildings at cost	100,000	
Furniture and fittings at cost	4,800	
Motor vehicles at cost	32,700	
Computer at cost	2,850	
Accumulated depreciation – buildings		6,000
Accumulated depreciation – furniture and fittings		2,880
Accumulated depreciation – motor vehicles		15,305
Accumulated depreciation – computer		1,900
Inventory at 1 April 20X3	4,400	
Bank/cash	3,960	
Petty cash	100	
Sales ledger control	15,000	
Purchases ledger control		5,010
Capital		130,000
Sales revenue		155,020
Sales returns	2,100	
Purchases	80,200	
Purchases returns		1,300
Bank charges	200	
Discounts allowed	1,060	
Discounts received		1,260
Wages	32,780	
Rates	6,000	
Telephone	1,140	
Electricity	1,480	
Insurance	1,200	
Motor expenses	1,380	
Office expenses	1,160	
Allowance for doubtful debts		300
Loan		820
Drawings	15,800	
Suspense	–	
Depreciation charge – building	2,000	
Depreciation charge – furniture and fittings	960	
Depreciation charge – motor vehicles	7,455	
Depreciation charge – computer	950	
Accruals		500
Prepayments	300	
Irrecoverable debts expense	240	
Allowance for doubtful debts adjustment	80	
Inventory – statement of financial position	5,200	
Inventory – statement of profit or loss		5,200
	325,495	325,495

Final ledger account adjustments

Once the balances on the trial balance have been taken to the statement of profit or loss and statement of financial position there is one final set of adjustments that must be done to some of the ledger accounts.

The income and expense ledger accounts must be closed off as the balances are no longer required in the ledger. This is done by taking the balances on each individual income and expense ledger account to a new ledger account known as the STATEMENT OF PROFIT OR LOSS LEDGER ACCOUNT.

HOW IT WORKS

The final balances on the sales revenue account, purchases account and wages account are shown below.

Sales revenue

	£		£
		Balance b/d	155,020

Purchases

	£		£
Balance b/d	80,200		

Wages

	£		£
Balance b/d	32,780		

These accounts must be closed off ready to start with a clean sheet at the beginning of the next accounting period. This is done by transferring the balances remaining to the statement of profit or loss ledger account.

Sales revenue

	£		£
Statement of profit or loss	155,020	Balance b/d	155,020

Purchases

	£		£
Balance b/d	80,200	Statement of profit or loss	80,200

Wages

	£		£
Balance b/d	32,780	Statement of profit or loss	32,780

Statement of profit or loss

	£		£
Purchases	80,200	Sales	155,020
Wages	32,780		

This will be done for all statement of profit or loss balances and there will need to be journal entries for each of these final adjustments. Therefore the final set of journal entries in full will be as follows:

Journal entries

	Debit	Credit
Opening inventory	£	£
Statement of profit or loss	4,400	
Inventory		4,400
Sales revenue		
Sales revenue	155,020	
Statement of profit or loss		155,020
Sales returns		
Statement of profit or loss	2,100	
Sales returns		2,100
Purchases		
Statement of profit or loss	80,200	
Purchases		80,200
Purchases returns		
Purchases returns	1,300	
Statement of profit or loss		1,300
Bank charges		
Statement of profit or loss	200	
Bank charges		200
Discounts allowed		
Statement of profit or loss	1,060	
Discounts allowed		1,060
Discounts received		
Discounts received	1,260	
Statement of profit or loss		1,260
Wages		
Statement of profit or loss	32,780	
Wages		32,780
Rates		
Statement of profit or loss	6,000	
Rates		6,000

	Debit £	Credit £
Telephone		
Statement of profit or loss	1,140	
Telephone		1,140
Electricity		
Statement of profit or loss	1,480	
Electricity		1,480
Insurance		
Statement of profit or loss	1,200	
Insurance		1,200
Motor expenses		
Statement of profit or loss	1,380	
Motor expenses		1,380
Office expenses		
Statement of profit or loss	1,160	
Office expenses		1,160
Depreciation charge – buildings		
Statement of profit or loss	2,000	
Depr'n charge – buildings		2,000
Depreciation charge – furniture and		
Statement of profit or loss	960	
Depr'n charge – furniture and fittings		960
Depreciation charge – motor vehicles		
Statement of profit or loss	7,455	
Depr'n charge – motor vehicles		7,455
Depreciation charge – computer		
Statement of profit or loss	950	
Depr'n charge – computer		950
Irrecoverable debt expense		
Statement of profit or loss	240	
Irrecoverable debts expense		240
Allowance for doubtful debts		
Statement of profit or loss	80	
Allowance for doubtful debts adjustment		80
Inventory – statement of profit or loss		
Inventory – statement of profit or loss	5,200	
Statement of profit or loss		5,200

Statement of financial position ledger account balances

There is no need to do any similar adjustments to statement of financial position ledger accounts ie assets and liabilities. This is because they remain as opening balances for the following accounting period in the ledger account. For example, the closing balance on the Buildings at cost account is £100,000 and this is the balance brought down or opening balance for the buildings at the start of the next accounting period.

Task 1

What are the year-end journal entries required to clear the following accounts:

(a)   Purchases returns account

Account name	Debit (✓)	Credit (✓)

(b)   Insurance account

Account name	Debit (✓)	Credit (✓)

(c)   Sales ledger control account

Account name	Debit (✓)	Credit (✓)

Task 2

Which of the following is an example of an error of commission where no control account is kept?

A   A receipt of £25 from J Gee entered in G Jay's account as a credit and debited to cash

B   A purchase of cleaning materials recorded as DR cash £50, CR cleaning materials £50

C   An invoice for £1,300 is lost and not recorded at all

D   An invoice for £2,500 sales is posted as £2,050

Task 3

Which of the following errors would be a possible reason for the trial balance not balancing?

A   Sales of £500 entered correctly but entered as £1,500 in the sales ledger control account

B   A purchase of £550 on credit not being recorded

C   Cash wages being recorded as DR cash £250, CR wages £250

D   A non-current asset purchase of £750 being recorded ad DR machinery repairs £750, CR cash £750

CHAPTER OVERVIEW

- Start by preparing an initial trial balance from the closing ledger account balances – you may need to set up a suspense account balance if the trial balance does not initially balance

- The suspense account must be cleared by journal entries to correct any errors identified

- Make journal entries for the period end adjustments for depreciation, accruals, prepayments, irrecoverable and doubtful debts and closing inventory

- Update the ledger account balances for the adjustments and corrections and prepare a final trial balance

- As a final year end adjustment all income and expense balances must be cleared out to the statement of profit or loss ledger account

TEST YOUR LEARNING

Test 1

The phone expense and insurance expense accounts of a sole trader have balances of £3,400 and £1,600 respectively at 30 September. However £300 of phone expense is to be accrued and £200 of insurance has been prepaid. What are the final expense figures that will appear in the statement of profit or loss for the year to 30 September?

Phone expense   £ [   ]

Insurance expense   £ [   ]

chapter 12:
THE EXTENDED TRIAL BALANCE

chapter coverage 📖

Accounts Preparation requires you to use the extended trial balance in order to help prepare the financial statements. This technique builds on the trial balance and the preparation of adjustments in order to let us see whether balances are going into the statement of profit or loss or the statement of financial position. It also helps in the calculation of the period's profit or loss. The topics covered in this chapter are:

✍ Extended trial balance

✍ Disposals and the ETB

EXTENDED TRIAL BALANCE

In this chapter we introduce the EXTENDED TRIAL BALANCE. The extended trial balance (ETB) is a technique that allows the initial trial balance to be adjusted for the necessary year end adjustments, to be corrected for any errors that are found and eventually to form the basis for the preparation of the financial statements.

An extended trial balance will normally have a column for the account name followed by eight further working columns:

Extended trial balance

Account name	Ledger balances		Adjustments		Statement of profit or loss		Statement of financial position	
	DR	CR	DR	CR	DR	CR	DR	CR

HOW TO PREPARE THE EXTENDED TRIAL BALANCE

We will start with a summary of the procedure for preparing an extended trial balance (ETB) and then work through it on a step by step basis.

Step 1   Enter each ledger account balance as either a debit or a credit in the ledger balance column. This is the initial trial balance and it should balance – however if there is a difference between the debits and the credits a suspense account balance should be added to make the trial balance add up. Leave a number of empty lines at the bottom of this trial balance before totalling it as these will be necessary for adjustments and corrections.

Step 2   If there is a suspense account, deal with the errors that have caused this by entering the debits and credits to correct the errors in the adjustments column.

Step 3   Enter any year end adjustments as directed in the adjustments column such as: the depreciation charge for the year, closing inventory, accruals and prepayments, irrecoverable debts written off and adjustments for allowance for doubtful debts. When doing this you may need to open up some new account lines in the ETB in the blank lines that you have left at the bottom of the ETB.

Step 4   Total and extend each line of the ETB into the statement of profit or loss or statement of financial position columns as appropriate.

Step 5   Total the statement of profit or loss columns. The difference is the profit or loss for the year. Enter this amount twice:

- In the appropriate column to make the statement of profit or loss columns balance and

- In the opposite statement of financial position column then

- Total the statement of financial position columns – they should be equal

HOW IT WORKS

We will use the example of John Thompson used in Chapter 11.

Given below is the list of ledger balances for John Thompson, a wholesaler of small electrical items, at his year end of 31 March 20X4.

	£
Buildings at cost	100,000
Furniture and fittings at cost	4,800
Motor vehicles at cost	32,700
Computer at cost	2,850
Accumulated depreciation at 1 April 20X3	
– buildings	4,000
– furniture and fittings	1,920
– motor vehicles	7,850
– computer	950
Inventory at 1 April 20X3	4,400
Bank/cash (debit balance)	3,960
Petty cash	100
Sales ledger control	15,240
Purchases ledger control	5,010
Capital	130,000
Sales revenue	155,020
Sales returns	2,100
Purchases	80,200
Purchases returns	1,400
Bank charges	200
Discounts allowed	890
Discounts received	1,260
Wages	32,780
Rates	5,500
Telephone	1,140
Electricity	1,480
Insurance	1,500
Motor expenses	1,580
Office expenses	960
Allowance for doubtful debts at 1 April 20X3	220
Loan	820
Drawings	15,800

Step 1   Enter these balances onto the ETB in the debit and credit columns of the ledger balance columns. Total the trial balance and check your totals carefully. Enter a suspense account balance if necessary.

Extended trial balance

Account name	Ledger balances DR £	Ledger balances CR £	Adjustments DR £	Adjustments CR £	SPL DR £	SPL CR £	SFP DR £	SFP CR £
Buildings at cost	100,000							
Furniture and fittings at cost	4,800							
Motor vehicles at cost	32,700							
Computer at cost	2,850							
Accumulated depreciation at 1 April 20X3:								
– buildings		4,000						
– furniture and fittings		1,920						
– motor vehicles		7,850						
– computer		950						
Inventory at 1 April 20X3	4,400							
Bank/cash	3,960							
Petty cash	100							
Sales ledger control	15,240							
Purchases ledger control		5,010						
Capital		130,000						
Sales revenue		155,020						
Sales returns	2,100							
Purchases	80,200							
Purchases returns		1,400						
Bank charges	200							
Discounts allowed	890							
Discounts received		1,260						
Wages	32,780							
Rates	5,500							
Telephone	1,140							
Electricity	1,480							
Insurance	1,500							
Motor expenses	1,580							
Office expenses	960							
Allowance for doubtful debts at 1 April 20X3		220						
Loan		820						
Drawings	15,800							
Suspense account	270							
	308,450	308,450						

In this case the trial balance does not balance. The total of the debit column is £308,180 and the total of the credit column is £308,450, so a suspense account balance of £270 is entered into the debit column in order to make the trial balance add up.

Take note of some of the entries in the trial balance. The accumulated depreciation and allowance for doubtful debts are as at 1 April 20X3. This means that the depreciation charge for the year has not yet been accounted for, nor has there been any adjustment to the allowance for receivables for the year.

The inventory figure in the trial balance is also as at 1 April 20X3, as it is the opening inventory. The inventory figure in the trial balance is always the opening inventory figure as the closing inventory is not entered into the accounts until the year end when it is counted and valued (see Chapter 7).

Step 2   Deal with the errors that have caused the balance on the suspense account. The errors that have been found are given below:

- The purchases returns account was overcast by £100

| Debit | Purchases returns | £100 |
| Credit | Suspense | £100 |

- £200 of office expenses has been charged to the motor expenses account

| Debit | Office expenses | £200 |
| Credit | Motor expenses | £200 |

- Discounts allowed of £170 had been correctly accounted for in the sales ledger control account but omitted from the discounts allowed account

| Debit | Discounts allowed | £170 |
| Credit | Suspense | £170 |

These three double entries will now be entered into the ETB.

Account name	Ledger balances		Adjustments		SPL		SFP	
	DR	CR	DR	CR	DR	CR	DR	CR
	£	£	£	£	£	£	£	£
Buildings at cost	100,000							
Furniture and fittings at cost	4,800							
Motor vehicles at cost	32,700							
Computer at cost	2,850							
Accumulated depreciation at 1 April 20X3:								
– buildings		4,000						
– furniture and fittings		1,920						
– motor vehicles		7,850						
– computer		950						
Inventory at 1 April 20X3	4,400							
Bank/cash	3,960							
Petty cash	100							
Sales ledger control	15,240							
Purchases ledger control		5,010						
Capital		130,000						
Sales revenue		155,020						
Sales returns	2,100							
Purchases	80,200							
Purchases returns		1,400	100					
Bank charges	200							
Discounts allowed	890		170					
Discounts received		1,260						
Wages	32,780							
Rates	5,500							
Telephone	1,140							
Electricity	1,480							
Insurance	1,500							
Motor expenses	1,580			200				
Office expenses	960		200					
Allowance for doubtful debts at 1 April 20X3		220						
Loan		820						
Drawings	15,800							
Suspense account	270			100 + 170				
	308,450	308,450						

Step 3   Enter the year end adjustments in the adjustments columns:

(a)   Depreciation

    (i)   Buildings – 2% straight line

         £100,000 × 2% = £2,000

Debit	Buildings depreciation charge	£2,000
Credit	Buildings accumulated depreciation	£2,000

    (ii)   Furniture and fittings – 20% straight line

         £4,800 × 20% = £960

Debit	Furniture depreciation charge	£960
Credit	Furniture accumulated depreciation	£960

    (iii)   Motor vehicles – 30% reducing balance

         (£32,700 – 7,850) × 30% = £7,455

Debit	Vehicles depreciation charge	£7,455
Credit	Vehicles accumulated depreciation	£7,455

    (iv)   Computer – 33⅓ % straight line

         £2,850 × 33⅓ % = £950

Debit	Computer depreciation charge	£950
Credit	Computer accumulated depreciation	£950

(b)   Rates of £500 are to be accrued

Debit	Rates	£500
Credit	Accruals	£500

(c)   The insurance account includes an amount of £300 prepaid

Debit	Prepayments	£300
Credit	Insurance	£300

(d)   An irrecoverable debt of £240 is to be written off

Debit	Irrecoverable debts expense	£240
Credit	Sales ledger control	£240

(e) An allowance for 2% of the remaining receivables (debtors) is to be made

   Allowance required 2% × (£15,240 – 240)   = £300
   Balance on allowance account at start of the year   = £220
   Increase in allowance required £300 – 220   = £80

   Debit   Allowance for doubtful debts adjustment   £80
   Credit   Allowance for doubtful debts   £80

(f) Closing inventory at 31 March 20X4 has been valued at £5,200

   Debit   Inventory account – statement of financial   £5,200
            position
   Credit   Inventory account – statement of profit or loss   £5,200

In the adjustment column of the ETB the entries to make are both a debit and a credit entry against the opening inventory line with the value of the closing inventory.

At this stage you have completed the adjustments. Therefore to check that all of the adjustments have consisted of complete double entry you should total the debit and credit adjustment columns – they should be equal.

Account name	Ledger balances DR £	Ledger balances CR £	Adjustments DR £	Adjustments CR £	SPL DR £	SPL CR £	SFP DR £	SFP CR £
Buildings at cost	100,000							
Furniture and fittings at cost	4,800							
Motor vehicles at cost	32,700							
Computer at cost	2,850							
Accumulated depreciation at 1 April 20X3:								
– buildings		4,000		2,000				
– furniture and fittings		1,920		960				
– motor vehicles		7,850		7,455				
– computer		950		950				
Inventory at 1 April 20X3	4,400		5,200	5,200				
Bank	3,960							
Petty cash	100							
Sales ledger control	15,240			240				
Purchases ledger control		5,010						
Capital		130,000						
Sales revenue		155,020						
Sales returns	2,100							
Purchases	80,200							
Purchases returns		1,400	100					
Bank charges	200							
Discounts allowed	890		170					
Discounts received		1,260						
Wages	32,780							
Rates	5,500		500					
Telephone	1,140							
Electricity	1,480							
Insurance	1,500			300				
Motor expenses	1,580			200				
Office expenses	960		200					
Allowance for doubtful debts at 1 April 20X3		220		80				
Loan		820						
Drawings	15,800							
Suspense account	270			100 + 170				
Buildings depreciation charge			2,000					
Furniture depreciation charge			960					
Motor vehicles depreciation charge			7,455					

Account name	Ledger balances		Adjustments		SPL		SFP	
	DR	CR	DR	CR	DR	CR	DR	CR
	£	£	£	£	£	£	£	£
Computer depreciation charge			950					
Accruals				500				
Prepayments			300					
Irrecoverable debts expense			240					
Allowance for doubtful debts adjustment			80					
	308,450	308,450	18,155	18,155				

Step 4   Total and extend each line of the ETB into the statement of profit or loss or statement of financial position columns as appropriate.

The approach here is to take each line in turn and firstly add it across, then decide whether this is a statement of profit or loss balance or a statement of financial position balance. As examples:

- The buildings at cost account has a debit balance of £100,000 in the ledger balances column – there are no entries in the adjustment column so the only decision to make is whether this £100,000 is a debit in the statement of profit or loss or the statement of financial position – it is of course a non-current asset that will appear in the debit column in the statement of financial position.

- The accumulated depreciation for buildings has a credit of £4,000 in the ledger balance column and a further credit of £2,000 in the adjustment column – this totals to a credit of £6,000. This is the accumulated depreciation and therefore it is a statement of financial position figure – this £6,000 is therefore taken across to the credit column of the statement of financial position.

- Inventory is a complicated one – there are three figures that need to be extended across:
    - Opening inventory of £4,400 (the debit balance in the ledger balances column) is taken to the debit of the statement of profit or loss
    - The debit in the adjustment column is taken as a debit to the statement of financial position, being the closing inventory current asset

  - The credit in the adjustment column is taken as a credit in the statement of profit or loss, being the reduction in purchases cost in the cost of sales

- The sales ledger control account has a debit balance in the ledger balances column of £15,240 and a credit of £240 in the adjustment column – therefore the credit of £240 is deducted from the debit of £15,240 to give a debit total of £15,000 which is taken to the debit column of the statement of financial position.

- The suspense account has a debit of £270 in the ledger balances column – there are two credit entries in the adjustment column which total to £270 therefore meaning that there is no balance to be extended across.

- The credit entry for accruals and the debit entry for prepayments are both taken across to the statement of financial position.

Now work carefully through the fully extended ETB ensuring that you are happy with each total and that you understand why the balances appear in the statement of profit or loss columns or the statement of financial position columns.

Remember:

Statement of profit or loss	–	income
	–	expenses
Statement of financial position	–	assets
	–	liabilities
	–	capital

Account name	Ledger balances DR £	CR £	Adjustments DR £	CR £	SPL DR £	CR £	SFP DR £	CR £
Buildings at cost	100,000						100,000	
Furniture and fittings at cost	4,800						4,800	
Motor vehicles at cost	32,700						32,700	
Computer at cost	2,850						2,850	
Accumulated depreciation at 1 April 20X3:								
– buildings		4,000		2,000				6,000
– furniture and fittings		1,920		960				2,880
– motor vehicles		7,850		7,455				15,305
– computer		950		950				1,900
Inventory at 1 April 20X3	4,400		5,200	5,200	4,400	5,200	5,200	
Bank/cash	3,960						3,960	
Petty cash	100						100	
Sales ledger control	15,240			240			15,000	
Purchases ledger control		5,010						5,010
Capital		130,000						130,000
Sales revenue		155,020				155,020		
Sales returns	2,100				2,100			
Purchases	80,200				80,200			
Purchases returns		1,400	100			1,300		
Bank charges	200				200			
Discounts allowed	890		170		1,060			
Discounts received		1,260				1,260		
Wages	32,780				32,780			
Rates	5,500		500		6,000			
Telephone	1,140				1,140			
Electricity	1,480				1,480			
Insurance	1,500			300	1,200			
Motor expenses	1,580			200	1,380			
Office expenses	960		200		1,160			
Allowance for doubtful debts at 1 April 20X3		220		80				300
Loan		820						820
Drawings	15,800						15,800	
Suspense account	270			100 + 170				
Buildings depreciation charge			2,000		2,000			
Furniture depreciation charge			960		960			
Motor vehicles depreciation charge			7,455		7,455			
Computer depreciation charge			950		950			
Accruals				500				500
Prepayments			300				300	
Irrecoverable debts expense			240		240			
Allowance for doubtful debts adjustment			80		80			
	308,450	308,450	18,155	18,155				

Step 5   Total the statement of profit or loss columns to find the profit or loss for the year:

- If the credits in the statement of profit of loss exceed the debits then there is more income than expense, so a profit has been made. This is the balancing debit in the statement of profit or loss and it requires a new account line of profit/loss. This same figure is also a credit in the statement of financial position columns (because it is adding to the owner's capital, which is always a credit balance).

- If the debits in the statement of profit or loss exceed the credits then there are more expenses than income and a loss has been made. This is the balancing credit in the statement of profit or loss (again this uses the new account line of profit/loss). This same figure is entered as a debit in the statement of financial position columns (because it is reducing the owner's capital).

Total the statement of financial position columns – they should be equal.

Account name	Ledger balance DR £	Ledger balance CR £	Adjusments DR £	Adjusments CR £	Statement of profit or loss DR £	Statement of profit or loss CR £	Statement of financial position DR £	Statement of financial position CR £
Building at cost	100,000						100,000	
Furniture and fittings at cost	4,800						4,800	
Motor vehicles at cost	32,700						32,700	
Computer at cost	2,850						2,850	
Accumulated depreciation at 1 April 2013:								
– buildings		4,000		2,000				6,000
– furniture and fittings		1,920		960				2,880
– motor vehicles		7,850		7,455				15,305
– computer		950		950				1,900
Stock (inventory) at 1 April 20X3	4,400		5,200	5,200	4,400	5,200	5,200	
Bank	3,960						3,960	
Petty cash	100						100	
Sales ledger control	15,240			240			15,000	
Purchases ledger control		5,010						5,010
Capital		130,000						130,000
Sales revenue		155,020				155,020		
Sales return	2,100				2,100			
Purchases	80,000				80,000			
Purchases returns		1,400	100			1,300		
Bank charges	200				200			

Account name	Ledger balance DR £	Ledger balance CR £	Adjustments DR £	Adjustments CR £	Statement of profit or loss DR £	Statement of profit or loss CR £	Statement of financial position DR £	Statement of financial position CR £
Discounts allowed	890		170		1,060			
Discounts received		1,260				1,260		
Wages	32,780				32,780			
Rates	5,500		500		6,000			
Telephone	1,140				1,140			
Electricity	1,480				1,480			
Insurance	1,500			300	1,200			
Motor expenses	1,580			200	1,380			
Office expenses	960		200		1,160			
Allowance for doubtful debts at 1 April 20X3		220		80				300
Loan		820						820
Drawings	15,800						15,800	
Suspense account	270			100 170				
Buildings depreciation charge			2,000		2,000			
Furniture depreciation charge			960		960			
Motor vehicles depreciation charge			7,455		7,455			
Computer depreciation charge			950		950			
Accruals				500				500
Prepayments			300				300	
Irrecoverable debts expense			240		240			
Allowance for doubtful debts adjustment			80		80			
Profit/loss					17,995			17,995
	308,450	308,450	18,155	18,155	162,780	162,780	180,710	180,710

In this case a profit of £17,995 was made. This is the balancing figure in the statement of profit or loss columns and is shown as a credit in the statement of financial position, to be added to the capital for the period.

Once it is entered into the credit column in the statement of financial position the statement of financial position columns should be totalled and the two column totals should be equal.

Task 1

If the credit balances exceed the debit balances in the statement of profit or loss columns this means the business has made a | profit/loss | for the period. The other entry to be made with this balancing amount is in |the debit column/credit column | of the statement of financial position.

DISPOSALS AND THE ETB

When a business disposes of a non-current asset and a profit or loss on disposal arises, the ETB can be used to process the journals necessary for this, calculate the profit or loss on disposal and allocate it correctly in the statement of profit or loss columns.

HOW IT WORKS

Adam Singleton operates a very simple business and his trial balance as at 31 December is as follows:

Ledger account	Dr £	Cr £
Capital		5,000
Sales revenue		15,000
Purchases	7,000	
Sales ledger control	6,000	
Purchases ledger control		2,000
Bank/cash	5,000	
Machine at cost	10,000	
Machine accumulated depreciation		6,000
	28,000	28,000

After the extraction of the trial balance on 31 December Adam disposed of the machine in return for a cheque for £3,500.

We need to adjust for this transaction and extend the ETB to arrive at Adam's profit for the period.

Step 1   Prepare journal entries for the disposal:

Account name	Amount £	Debit (✓)	Credit (✓)
Disposals	10,000	✓	
Machine at cost	10,000		✓
Machine accumulated depreciation	6,000	✓	
Disposals	6,000		✓
Bank/cash	3,500	✓	
Disposals	3,500		✓

Step 2   Next we process these adjustments on the ETB:

Extended trial balance as at 31 December

	Ledger balances DR £	Ledger balances CR £	Adjustments DR £	Adjustments CR £	SPL DR £	SPL CR £	SFP DR £	SFP CR £
Capital		5,000						
Sales revenue		15,000						
Purchases	7,000							
Sales ledger control	6,000							
Purchases ledger control		2,000						
Bank/cash	5,000		3,500					
Machine at cost	10,000			10,000				
Machine acc depreciation		6,000	6,000					
Disposals			10,000	6,000				
				3,500				
	28,000	28,000	19,500	19,500				

Step 3   Debits exceed credits by £500 on the disposal line of the ETB, so we know that the disposal has been at a £500 loss. This amount is entered in the debit column of the statement of profit or loss, so the disposals line now cross casts.

Extended trial balance as at 31 December

	Ledger balances DR £	Ledger balances CR £	Adjustments DR £	Adjustments CR £	SPL DR £	SPL CR £	SFP DR £	SFP CR £
Capital		5,000						
Sales revenue		15,000						
Purchases	7,000							
Sales ledger control	6,000							
Purchases ledger control		2,000						
Bank/cash	5,000		3,500					
Machine at cost	10,000			10,000				
Machine acc depreciation		6,000	6,000					
Disposals			10,000	6,000	500			
				3,500				
Profit								
	28,000	28,000	19,500	19,500	500			

Step 4 The remainder of the balances are also extended, and the statement of profit or loss columns are totalled:

Extended trial balance as at 31 December

Ledger account	Ledger balances DR £	Ledger balances CR £	Adjustments DR £	Adjustments CR £	SPL DR £	SPL CR £	SFP DR £	SFP CR £
Capital		5,000						5,000
Sales revenue		15,000				15,000		
Purchases	7,000				7,000			
Sales ledger control	6,000						6,000	
Purchases ledger control		2,000						2,000
Bank/cash	5,000		3,500				8,500	
Machine at cost	10,000			10,000				
Machine acc depreciation		6,000	6,000					
Disposals			10,000	6,000	500			
				3,500				
Profit								
	28,000	8,000	19,500	19,500	7,500	15,000		

Step 5 The profit for the year of £7,500 is entered on the debit side of the statement of profit or loss, to make it balance, and on the credit side of the statement of financial position, again to make it balance. The statement of profit or loss and statement of financial position columns are then totalled, and should balance.

Extended trial balance as at 31 December

	Ledger balances		Adjustments		SPL		SFP	
	DR £	CR £	DR £	CR £	DR £	CR £	DR £	CR £
Capital		5,000						5,000
Sales revenue		15,000				15,000		
Purchases	7,000				7,000			
Sales ledger control	6,000						6,000	
Purchases ledger control		2,000						2,000
Bank/cash	5,000		3,500				8,500	
Machine at cost	10,000			10,000				
Machine acc dep		6,000	6,000					
Disposals			10,000	6,000	500			
				3,500				
Profit					7,500			7,500
	28,000	28,000	19,500	19,500	15,000	15,000	14,500	14,500

Task 2

The following balances have been taken from the trial balance of XYZ. Rent paid £1,800, capital £15,000, purchases £10,000, sales revenue £12,000, wages £5,000, sundry expenses £1,000, cash £9,200. What is the trial balance total on the debit side?

A £26,000

B £29,000

C £42,000

D £27,000

Task 3

A suspense account shows a credit balance of £130. This could be due to:

A Omitting a sale of £130 from the sales ledger.

B Recording a purchase of £130 twice in the purchases account.

C Failing to write off an irrecoverable debt of £130.

D Recording an electricity bill paid of £65 by debiting the bank account and crediting the electricity account.

CHAPTER OVERVIEW

- Once the initial trial balance has been prepared any errors that have caused a suspense account and any year end adjustments are put through the accounts in order to arrive at the figures for the final accounts – this can all be done in the extended trial balance

- The first stage is to enter all of the ledger account balances into the ETB and to check that it balances – if it does not balance then a suspense account is entered in order to create a balanced trial balance

- The suspense account is then cleared by entering the correcting entries in the adjustments columns of the ETB

- Any year end adjustments are then also entered in the adjustment columns for depreciation, irrecoverable and doubtful debts and accruals and prepayments

- The closing inventory figure is entered as a debit and a credit entry in the adjustment columns on the inventory line

- Each line of the ETB is then totalled and extended into either the statement of profit or loss columns or the statement of financial position columns as a debit or a credit – in the statement of profit or loss there are income and expenses – in the statement of financial position there are assets, liabilities and capital

- The statement of profit or loss columns are then totalled and the balancing figure is inserted as a new account line, the profit/loss, which is also inserted in the statement of financial position columns – a debit in the statement of profit or loss column is a credit in the statement of financial position column and *vice versa*

- The final stage is to total the statement of financial position columns and these should now agree

Keyword

Extended trial balance – an accounting technique of moving from the trial balance, through the year end adjustments to the figures for the final accounts

TEST YOUR LEARNING

Test 1

When preparing an extended trial balance what do you do if you discover that the initial trial balance does not balance?

Test 2

What entries if any are made in the adjustments column for the closing inventory?

Both a debit and a credit

A debit

A credit

No entry

Test 3

The closing inventory figure is a $\boxed{\text{debit entry/credit entry}}$ in the statement of profit or loss columns and a $\boxed{\text{debit entry/credit entry}}$ in the statement of financial position columns of the ETB.

ANSWERS TO CHAPTER TASKS

CHAPTER 1 **Accounting principles**

1 a receivable
2 a credit note
3 the purchases day book
4 the purchases ledger

5

Sales ledger control account

Date	Details	Amount £	Date	Details	Amount £
4 Mar	Sales revenue	2,400			

Sales revenue

Date	Details	Amount £	Date	Details	Amount £
			4 Mar	Receivables	2,400

Purchases

Date	Details	Amount £	Date	Details	Amount £
4 Mar	Payables	1,800			

Purchases ledger control account

Date	Details	Amount £	Date	Details	Amount £
			4 Mar	Purchases	1,800

Phone

Date	Details	Amount £	Date	Details	Amount £
4 Mar	Bank/cash	140			

Bank/cash

Date	Details	Cash £	Bank £	Date	Details	Cash £	Bank £
				4 Mar	Phone		140
				4 Mar	Drawings		500

Drawings

Date	Details	Amount £	Date	Details	Amount £
4 Mar	Bank/cash	500			

6

Sales ledger control account

Date	Details	Amount £	Date	Details	Amount £
17 Feb	Sales revenue	900	25 Feb	Bank/cash	700
			28 Feb	Bal c/d	200
	Total	900		Total	900
1 Mar	Bal b/d	200			

7 The correct answer is **B**

If the bookkeeping has been accurate, the total of the debits will equal the total of the credits in the trial balance.

CHAPTER 2 Accounting concepts

1

	£	Description
Rent	480	Expense
Motor van	7,400	Asset
Payables	1,900	Liability
Heat and light	210	Expense
Discounts received	50	Income
Motor expenses	310	Expense
Sales revenue	40,800	Income
Opening inventory	2,100	Asset
Loan	2,000	Liability
Stationery	330	Expense
Capital	7,980	Capital
Phone	640	Expense
Discount allowed	60	Expense
Purchases	22,600	Expense
Receivables	3,400	Asset
Wages	9,700	Expense
Drawings	4,000	Reduction of capital
Office cleaning	220	Expense
Travel and accommodation	660	Expense
Bank	483	Asset
Cash	137	Asset

2

	£	£
Sales revenue		136,700
Less: cost of sales		
Opening inventory	11,300	
Purchases	97,500	
	108,800	
Less: closing inventory	(10,600)	
		98,200
Gross profit		38,500

3

	Debit	Credit	Statement of profit or loss	Statement of financial position
	£	£		
Rent	480		✓	
Motor van	7,400			✓
Payables		1,900		✓
Heat and light	210		✓	
Discounts received		50	✓	
Motor expenses	310		✓	
Sales revenue		40,800	✓	
Opening inventory	2,100		✓	
Loan		2,000		✓
Stationery	330		✓	
Capital		7,980		✓
Phone	640		✓	
Discount allowed	60		✓	
Purchases	22,600		✓	
Receivables	3,400			✓
Wages	9,700		✓	
Drawings	4,000			✓
Office cleaning	220		✓	
Travel and accommodation	660		✓	
Bank	483			✓
Cash	137			✓
	52,730	52,730		

4   Accruals

CHAPTER 3 **Purchase of non-current assets**

1 Capital expenditure £15,000

Revenue expenditure £4,000

Expenditure on Machine A is capital expenditure as it is a major improvement of the asset. The £4,000 repair costs of Machine B is revenue expenditure as this is just the running costs of the machine.

2

Machinery account

	£		£
Purchases ledger control	17,000		
Wages	1,400		

Purchases ledger control account

	£		£
		Machinery	17,000

Wages account

	£		£
		Machinery	1,400

3

Account	Amount £	Debit	Credit
Motor vehicles	78,800	✓	
Motor expenses	800	✓	
Bank account	79,600		✓

4

Account name	Amount £	Debit	Credit
Motor vehicles	25,000	✓	
Bank / cash	15,000		✓
Disposals	10,000		✓
Being the purchase of a new car for cash / part exchange.			

CHAPTER 4 Depreciation of non-current assets

1   Carrying amount = Cost – depreciation to date

Carrying amount = £8,000 – £3,000 = £5,000

2   Depreciation charge $= \dfrac{£22,000 - 9,000}{4}$

$= £3,250$ per annum

Carrying amount $= £22,000 - (2 \times 3,250) = £15,500$

3

	£
Original cost	22,000
Year 1 depreciation 22,000 × 20%	(4,400)
Carrying amount at end of year 1	17,600
Year 2 depreciation 17,600 × 20%	(3,520)
Carrying amount at end of year 2	14,080
Year 3 depreciation 14,080 × 20%	(2,816)
Carrying amount at end of year 3	11,264
Year 4 depreciation 11,264 × 20%	(2,253)
Carrying amount	9,011

4

Depreciation charge

	£		£
Accumulated depreciation	24,000		

Accumulated depreciation

	£		£
		Depreciation charge	24,000

Statement of profit or loss

	£
Expenses:	
Depreciation charge	24,000

SFP

Non-current assets:

	Cost	Depreciation	Carrying amount
	£	£	£
Machinery	120,000	24,000	96,000

5   False

The diminishing balance method results in larger amounts being charged in earlier years and smaller amounts in subsequent years.

CHAPTER 5   Disposal of non-current assets

1

(a)

	£
Original cost	11,200
20X7 depreciation 11,200 × 30%	3,360
Carrying amount 31 Dec 20X7	7,840
20X8 depreciation 7,840 × 30%	2,352
Carrying amount 31 Dec 20X8	5,488

(b)

Carrying amount at 31 December 20X8	5,488
Disposal proceeds	5,000
Loss on disposal	488

(c)

Motor car at cost account

	£		£
1 Jan 20X7 Bank	11,200	31 Dec 20X8 Disposal	11,200

Accumulated depreciation on the motor car account

	£		£
31 Dec 20X7 Balance c/d	3,360	31 Dec 20X7 Depreciation	3,360
31 Dec 20X8 Disposal	5,712	1 Jan 20X8 Balance b/d	3,360
		31 Dec 20X8 Depreciation	2,352
	5,712		5,712

Disposals account

	£		£
31 Dec 20X8 Motor car at cost	11,200	31 Dec 20X8 Motor car accumulated depreciation	5,712
		31 Dec 20X8 Proceeds	5,000
		31 Dec 20X8 SPL – loss	88
	11,200		11,200

2

Car at cost account

	£		£
1 Mar 20X6 Bank/cash	10,000	31 May 20X8 Disposals	10,000
31 May 20X8 Bank/cash	6,200	31 May 20X8 Balance c/d	11,000
31 May 20X8 Disposals	4,800		
	21,000		21,000
1 June 20X8 Balance b/d	11,000		

Car accumulated depreciation account

	£		£
31 May 20X8 Disposals	5,500	31 May 20X8 Balance b/d	5,500

Disposals account

	£		£
31 May 20X8 Car at cost	10,000	31 May 20X8 Car accumulated depreciation	5,500
31 May 20X8 SPL – profit on disposal	300	31 May 20X8 Car at cost	4,800
	10,300		10,300

3

Non-Current Asset Register

Non-current asset number	24116
Description	Fork lift truck XC355
Location	Warehouse
Supplier	Leyland Machinery

Date	Cost £	Expected life (years)	Estimated residual value £	Depreciation method	Depreciation rate	Depreciation charge for the year £	Acc dep at end of the year £	Carrying amount at end of year £	Disposal proceeds £	Profit or loss on disposal £
20X5										
1 May	34,000	4	6,250	Reducing balance	30%					
31 Dec						10,200	10,200	23,800		
20X6										
31 Dec						7,140	17,340	16,660		
20X7										
31 Dec						4,998	22,338	11,662		
20X8										
20 Mar									10,500	(1,162)

4   The correct answer is **D**.

CHAPTER 6   Accruals and prepayments

1   This will ⌐increase¬ phone expenses in the old accounting year, and it will be shown as ⌐a liability¬ on the statement of financial position at the year end.

2

Phone account

	£		£
31 Dec Balance b/d	2,600		
31 Dec Accrual c/d	480	31 Dec Statement of profit or loss	3,080
	3,080		3,080
		1 Jan Accrual b/d	480

3

Rent account

	£		£
31 Dec Balance b/d	3,200	31 Dec Statement of profit or loss	2,900
		31 Dec Prepayment c/d ($£900 \times 1/3$)	300
	3,200		3,200
1 Jan Prepayment b/d	300		

4   Asset

Accrued income is due but has not been received, therefore it is a form of asset.

CHAPTER 7 **Inventory**

1   Cost   =   £13.80

   Net realisable value   =   £14.00 – 0.50

                                  =   £13.50

   Each unit should be valued at £13.50, the lower of cost and net realisable value

2   12 May – sale –70 units @ £3.50

   30 May – sale – 80 units   30 units @ £3.50

                                        50 units @ £4.00

   Closing inventory – 50 units @ £4.00 = £200.00

3   The purchases account.

   The cost of goods purchased should **never** be debited to the inventory account. The inventory account is adjusted at the end of the accounting period only.

CHAPTER 8 Irrecoverable debts and doubtful debts

1

Account name	Debit £	Credit £
Irrecoverable debts expense	976	
Sales ledger control		976
Being the write-off of a specific receivable		

2

Account name	Debit £	Credit £
Bank/cash account	1,000	
Irrecoverable debts expense account		1,000
Being the recovery of a specific receivable previously written-off		

3

Account name	Debit £	Credit £
Irrecoverable debts expense	680	
Sales ledger control		680
Allowance for doubtful debts adjustment	630	
Allowance for doubtful debts		630
Being the write-off of one debt and the set-up of a new general allowance for doubtful debts		

4

Account name	Debit £	Credit £
Irrecoverable debts expense	2,400	
Sales ledger control		2,400
Allowance for doubtful debts	924	
Allowance for doubtful debts adjustment		924
Being write-off of irrecoverable debt and reduction of allowance for doubtful debts from £1,500 to ((£60,000 − £2,400) × 1%) = £576		

5

Account name	Debit £	Credit £
Allowance for doubtful debts (SFP)	√	
Allowance for doubtful debts adj (SPL)		√

6 Prudence.

CHAPTER 9   Bank reconciliations

1   £12,255

Workings	Debit £	Credit £
Balance per cash book	12,450	
Standing order for rent		400
BGC receipt from customer	230	
Bank charges		25
Adjusted cash book balance c/d		12,255
	12,680	12,680

2

Account name	Amount £	Debit (✓)	Credit (✓)
Sales ledger control account	500	√	
Cash book	500		√

3   The correct answer is **C**.

CHAPTER 10   **Control account reconciliations**

1

Account name	Debit £	Credit £
Purchases ledger control	500	
Sales ledger control		500
Being the setting off of sales ledger and purchases ledger balances		

2   The sales ledger control account but not the individual balances in the sales ledger.

3

Adjustment	Amount £	Debit (✓)	Credit (✓)
Sales ledger control	120		✓

The other side of the entry would be a debit to the discounts allowed account.

4

Adjustment	Amount £	Debit (✓)	Credit (✓)
Purchases ledger balances	700		✓

5   The correct answer is **D**.

6   The correct answer is **B**.

CHAPTER 11 **The trial balance, errors and the suspense account**

1 (a) Debit   Purchases returns
Credit   Statement of profit or loss

(b) Debit   Statement of profit or loss
Credit   Insurance

(c) No adjustment required as this is a statement of financial position item.

2 The correct answer is **A**.

3 The correct answer is **A**.

CHAPTER 12 **The extended trial balance**

1   This means that the business has made a **profit** for the period and the other entry is in the **credit column** of the statement of financial position.

2   The correct answer is **D.**

Workings:

	DR £	CR £
Rent	1,800	
Capital		15,000
Purchases	10,000	
Sales revenue		12,000
Wages	5,000	
Sundry expenses	1,000	
Cash	9,200	
	27,000	27,000

3   The correct answer is **B.**

£130 will be debited twice to purchases, giving rise to a credit balance in the suspense account.

CHAPTER 1   Accounting principles

1

Bank account

Date	Details	£	Date	Details	£
1/3	Capital	20,000	1/3	Furn & fit	3,200
10/3	Sales revenue	1,800	4/3	Purchases	4,400
24/3	Receivables	3,500	6/3	Rent	600
			28/3	Drawings	1,000
			30/3	Payables	1,800
			31/3	Wages	900
			31/3	Balance c/d	13,400
		25,300			25,300
1/4	Balance b/d	13,400			

Capital account

Date	Details	£	Date	Details	£
			1/3	Bank/cash	20,000

Furniture and fittings account

Date	Details	£	Date	Details	£
1/3	Bank/cash	3,200			

Purchases account

Date	Details	£	Date	Details	£
4/3	Bank/cash	4,400	31/3	Balance c/d	7,100
20/3	Payables	2,700			
		7,100			7,100
1/4	Balance b/d	7,100			

Rent account

Date	Details	£	Date	Details	£
6/3	Bank/cash	600			

Sales revenue account

Date	Details	£	Date	Details	£
31/3	Balance c/d	8,300	10/3	Bank/cash	1,800
			15/3	Receivables	4,900
			29/3	Receivables	1,600
		8,300			8,300
			1/4	Balance b/d	8,300

Sales ledger control account

Date	Details	£	Date	Details	£
15/3	Sales revenue	4,900	24/3	Bank/cash	3,500
29/3	Sales revenue	1,600	31/3	Balance c/d	3,000
		6,500			6,500
1/4	Balance b/d	3,000			

Purchases ledger control account

Date	Details	£	Date	Details	£
30/3	Bank/cash	1,800	20/3	Purchases	2,700
31/3	Balance c/d	900			
		2,700			2,700
			1/4	Balance b/d	900

Drawings account

Date	Details	£	Date	Details	£
28/3	Bank/cash	1,000			

Wages account

Date	Details	£	Date	Details	£
31/3	Bank/cash	900			

Trial balance as at 31 March

	Debits £	Credits £
Bank	13,400	
Capital		20,000
Furniture and fittings	3,200	
Purchases	7,100	
Rent	600	
Sales revenue		8,300
Receivables	3,000	
Payables		900
Drawings	1,000	
Wages	900	
	29,200	29,200

2 General ledger

Sales ledger control account

Date	Details	£	Date	Details	£
31 Mar	SDB	1,390	31 Mar	SRDB	60
			31 Mar	CRB	720
			31 Mar	CRB - discounts	10
			31 Mar	Balance c/d	600
		1,390			1,390
1 Apr	Balance b/d	600			

Sales revenue account

Date	Details	£	Date	Details	£
			31 Mar	SDB	1,390
31 Mar	Balance c/d	3,060	31 Mar	CRB	1,670
		3,060			3,060
			1 Apr	Balance b/d	3,060

Sales returns account

Date	Details	£	Date	Details	£
31 Mar	SRDB	60			

Purchases ledger control account

Date	Details	£	Date	Details	£
31 Mar	PRDB	80	31 Mar	PDB	1,400
31 Mar	CPB	870			
31 Mar	CPB – discounts	40			
31 Mar	Balance c/d	410			
		1,400			1,400
			1 Apr	Balance b/d	410

Purchases account

Date	Details	£	Date	Details	£
31 Mar	PDB	1,400			
31 Mar	CPB	2,250	31 Mar	Balance c/d	3,650
		3,650			3,650
1 Apr	Balance b/d	3,650			

Purchases returns account

Date	Details	£	Date	Details	£
			31 Mar	PRDB	80

Capital account

Date	Details	£	Date	Details	£
			31 Mar	CRB	15,000

Discounts allowed account

Date	Details	£	Date	Details	£
31 Mar	CRB	10			

Wages account

Date	Details	£	Date	Details	£
31 Mar	CPB	2,200			

Shop fittings account

Date	Details	£	Date	Details	£
31 Mar	CPB	1,100			

Discounts received account

Date	Details	£	Date	Details	£
			31 Mar	CPB	40

Bank/cash

Date	Details	£	Date	Details	£
31 Mar	CRB	17,390	31 Mar	CPB	6,420
			31 Mar	Balance c/d	10,970
		17,390			17,390
1 Apr	Balance b/d	10,970			

Sales ledger

J Simpson

Date	Details	£	Date	Details	£
4 Mar	SDB 0001	420	20 Mar	CRB	420

F Barnet

Date	Details	£	Date	Details	£
12 Mar	SDB 0002	350	19 Mar	SRDB CN 001	40
			31 Mar	CRB	300
			31 Mar	CRB – discount	10
		350			350

H Jerry

Date	Details	£	Date	Details	£
18 Mar	SDB 0003	180	25 Mar	SRDB CN 002	20
			31 Mar	Balance c/d	160
		180			180
1 Apr	Balance b/d	160			

D Dawson

Date	Details	£	Date	Details	£
28 Mar	SDB 0004	440			

Purchases ledger

L Lilley

Date	Details	£	Date	Details	£
12 Mar	CPB 0003	560	1 Mar	PDB 89432	590
12 Mar	CPD – discounts	30			
		590			590

O Rools

Date	Details	£	Date	Details	£
10 Mar	PRDB C357	80	7 Mar	PDB 12332	400
20 Mar	CPB	310			
20 Mar	CPB – discounts	10			
		400			400

R Terry

Date	Details	£	Date	Details	£
			24 Mar	PDB 0532	410

Trial balance as at 31 March

	Debits £	Credits £
Receivables	600	
Sales revenue		3,060
Sales returns	60	
Payables		410
Purchases	3,650	
Purchases returns		80
Capital		15,000
Discounts allowed	10	
Wages	2,200	
Shop fittings	1,100	
Discounts received		40
Bank/cash	10,970	
	18,590	18,590

CHAPTER 2   Accounting concepts

1

	Debit £	Credit £	Type of balance	SPL or SFP
Sales revenue		41,200	Income	SPL
Loan		1,500	Liability	SFP
Wages	7,000		Expense	SPL
Non-current assets	7,100		Asset	SFP
Opening inventory	1,800		Expense (see note)	SPL
Receivables	3,400		Asset	SFP
Discounts received		40	Income	SPL
Postage	100		Expense	SPL
Bank	300		Asset	SFP
Capital		9,530	Capital	SFP
Rent	500		Expense	SPL
Purchases	30,100		Expense	SPL
Payables		2,500	Liability	SFP
Discounts allowed	70		Expense	SPL
Drawings	3,000		Reduction of capital	SFP
Electricity	800		Expense	SPL
Telephone	600		Expense	SPL
	54,770	54,770		

Note   Opening inventory is included in the statement of profit or loss as part of the calculation of cost of sales. It is the closing inventory balance, which is an asset at the end of the accounting period, that is included in the statement of financial position.

2   (a)   The gross profit of a business is the profit from the **trading activities**.

(b)   The total of the current assets minus the current liabilities is known as **net current assets**.

3   (a)   Accruals concept

(b)   Going concern concept

(c)   Materiality concept

CHAPTER 3 **Purchase of non-current assets**

1 (a) Capital expenditure £15,700
Revenue expenditure £100

(b) Capital expenditure £61,100

(c) Capital expenditure £68,600
Revenue expenditure £800

2

	Account	Amount	Debit	Credit
		£		
(a)	Furniture and fittings	4,200	✓	
	Bank/cash	4,200		✓
	Being purchase of desks and chairs for head office			
(b)	Computers	2,300	✓	
	Computer expenses	100	✓	
	Purchases ledger control	2,400		✓
	Being purchase of computer and rewritable CDs			
(c)	Machinery	10,600	✓	
	Purchases	200		✓
	Wages	800		✓
	Bank/cash	9,600		✓
	Being purchase and installation of machine			

3 On the date of payment of the deposit

CHAPTER 4   Depreciation of non-current assets

1   The main accounting concept underlying the depreciation of non-current assets is the ⌑accruals⌑ concept.

2   Depreciation charge $= \dfrac{£11,500 - 2,500}{5 \text{ years}} = £1,800$ per annum

   Carrying amount at 31 December 20X8 = £11,500 – (2 × £1,800) = £7,900

3

	£
Original cost	16,400
Depreciation to 31 Dec 20X7 (16,400 × 35%)	5,740
Carrying amount at 31 Dec 20X7	10,660
Depreciation to 31 Dec 20X8 (10,660 × 35%)	3,731
Carrying amount at 31 Dec 20X8	6,929

4   Depreciation charge $=$ (£240,000 – £135,000) × 30%

   $=$ £31,500

5   Depreciation charge $=$ £24,000 × 20% × 7/12

   $=$ £2,800

CHAPTER 5   Disposal of non-current assets

1   (a)

	£
Original cost	2,200
20X5 depreciation 2,200 × 40%	880
20X5 carrying amount	1,320
20X6 depreciation 1,320 × 40%	528
20X6 carrying amount	792
20X7 depreciation 792 × 40%	317
20X7 carrying amount	475
Disposal proceeds	200
oss on disposal	275

)

Computer at cost account

Date	Details	£	Date	Details	£
1 April 20X5	Bank	2,200	14 May 20X8	Disposal	2,200

Computer accumulated depreciation account

Date	Details	£	Date	Details	£
31 Dec 20X5	Balance c/d	880	31 Dec 20X5	Expense	880
			1 Jan 20X6	Balance b/d	880
31 Dec 20X6	Balance c/d	1,408	31 Dec 20X6	Expense	528
		1,408			1,408
			1 Jan 20X7	Balance b/d	1,408
31 Dec 20X7	Balance c/d	1,725	31 Dec 20X7	Expense	317
		1,725			1,725
14 May 20X8	Disposal	1,725	1 Jan 20X8	Balance b/d	1,725

Disposals account

Date	Details	£	Date	Details	£
14 May 20X8	Cost	2,200	14 May 20X8	Depreciation	1,725
			14 May 20X8	Proceeds	200
			14 May 20X8	SPL – loss	275
		2,200			2,200

2 (a)

	£
Original cost	7,200
20X6 depreciation 7,200 × 25% × 2/12	(300)
20X7 depreciation 7,200 × 25%	(1,800)
20X8 depreciation 7,200 × 25% × 8/12	(1,200)
Carrying amount 31 July 20X8	3,900
Proceeds	(3,800)
Loss on disposal	100

(b)

Machine at cost account

Date	Details	£	Date	Details	£
1 Oct 20X6	Bank	7,200	31 July 20X8	Disposal	7,200

Machine accumulated depreciation account

Date	Details	£	Date	Details	£
30 Nov 20X6	Balance c/d	300	30 Nov 20X6	Expense	300
			1 Dec 20X6	Balance b/d	300
30 Nov 20X7	Balance c/d	2,100	30 Nov 20X7	Expense	1,800
		2,100			2,100
			1 Dec 20X7	Balance b/d	2,100
30 July 20X8	Disposal	3,300	31 July 20X8	Expense	1,200
		3,300			3,300

Disposals account

Date	Details	£	Date	Details	£
31 July 20X8	Cost	7,200	31 July 20X8	Depreciation	3,300
			31 July 20X8	Proceeds	3,800
			31 July 20X8	SPL – loss	100
		7,200			7,200

3 (a) A loss on disposal can also be described as **under-depreciation**.

(b) A profit on disposal can also be described as **over-depreciation**.

4

Van at cost account

Date	Details	£	Date	Details	£
1 July 20X5	Bank	13,600	30 Apr 20X8	Disposal	13,600
30 Apr 20X8	Bank	12,200			
30 Apr 20X8	Disposal				
	(16,700 – 12,200)	4,500	30 Apr 20X8	Balance c/d	16,700
		30,300			30,300

Van accumulated depreciation account

Date	Details	£	Date	Details	£
30 Apr 20X8	Disposal	9,000	30 Apr 20X8	Balance b/d	9,000

Disposals account

Date	Details	£	Date	Details	£
30 Apr 20X8	Cost	13,600	30 Apr 20X8	Depreciation	9,000
			30 Apr 20X8	Cost	4,500
			30 Apr 20X8	SPL – loss	100
		13,600			13,600

5

NON-CURRENT ASSET REGISTER
Non-current asset number 10435
Description Computer 1036525
Location Sales Department
Supplier **Timing Company Ltd**

Date	Cost £	Expected life (years)	Estimated residual value £	Depreciation method	Depreciation rate	Depreciation charge for the year £	Acc dep at end of the year £	Carrying amount at end of year £	Disposal proceeds £	Profit or loss on disposal £
20X6 1 Mar	4,800	4	600	Reducing balance	40%					
31 July						1,920	1,920	2,880		
20X7 31 July						1,152	3,072	1,728		
20X8 27 Jun									700	(1,028)

CHAPTER 6   Accruals and prepayments

1   (a)   Rent paid in advance for the following accounting period would appear as **a prepayment** in the statement of financial position.

   (b)   Motor expenses owing to the local garage would appear as **an accrual** in the statement of financial position.

2   (a)   In the statement of profit or loss the heat and light expense would be **£870**. In the statement of financial position there would be an **accrual** for **£200**.

   (b)   In the statement of profit or loss the rental income would be **£340**. In the statement of financial position there would be a **prepayment of income** of **£40**.

   (c)   In the statement of profit or loss the insurance expense would be **£1,100**. In the statement of financial position there would be a **prepayment** of **£300**.

   (d)   In the statement of profit or loss commissions income would be **£200**. In the statement of financial position there would be an **accrual of income** of **£20**.

3

Motor expenses account

Date	Details	£	Date	Details	£
30 June	Balance b/d	845	30 June	Prepayments c/d (150 × 6/12)	75
			30 June	Statement of profit or loss	770
		845			845
1 July	Prepayments b/d	75			

4

Electricity account

Date	Details	£	Date	Details	£
31 Mar	Balance b/d	470	31 Mar	Statement of profit or loss	650
31 Mar	Accruals c/d	180			
		650			650
			1 Apr	Accruals b/d	180

CHAPTER 7 **Inventory**

1 (a) Cost   =   £25.80 + 1.00 = £26.80

    NRV   =   £28.00 – 1.10 = £26.90

  (b) 120 × £26.80 = £3,216.00

CHAPTER 8 **Irrecoverable debts and doubtful debts**

1 General ledger

Sales ledger control account

	£		£
Balance b/d	25,673	Irrecoverable debts expense	445
		(157 + 288)	
		Balance c/d	25,228
	25,673		25,673
Balance b/d	25,228		

Irrecoverable debts expense account

	£		£
Sales ledger control	445	Statement of profit or loss	445

Sales ledger

H Taylor

	£		£
Balance b/d	157	Irrecoverable debts expense	157

C Phelps

	£		£
Balance b/d	288	Irrecoverable debts expense	288

2

Bank account

	£		£
Irrecoverable debts expense account	250		

Irrecoverable debts expense account

	£		£
		Bank account	250

3 (a)

	£
Sales ledger control account	11,650
Irrecoverable debt	(350)
	11,300
Specific allowance	(200)
Remaining receivables (debtors)	11,100
General allowance 2% × £11,100	222
Specific allowance	200
Total allowance for doubtful debts	422

(b)

Irrecoverable debts expense account

	£		£
Sales ledger control account	350	Statement of profit or loss	350

Sales ledger control account

	£		£
Balance b/d	11,650	Irrecoverable debts expense	350
		Balance c/d	11,300
	11,650		11,650
Balance b/d	11,300		

Allowance for doubtful debts adjustment account

	£		£
Allowance for doubtful debts	422	Statement of profit or loss	422

Allowance for doubtful debts account

	£		£
		Allowance for doubtful debts adjustment account	422

4

Irrecoverable debts expense account

		£			£
20X7			20X7		
31 Dec	Sales ledger control	370	31 Dec	Statement of profit or loss	370
20X8			20X8		
31 Dec	Sales ledger control	400	31 Dec	Statement of profit or loss	400

Allowance for doubtful debts adjustment account

		£			£
20X7			20X7		
31 Dec	Allowance for doubtful debts	228	31 Dec	Statement of profit or loss	228
20X8			20X8		
31 Dec	Statement of profit or loss	168	31 Dec	Allowance for doubtful debts	168

Allowance for doubtful debts account

		£			£
20X7			20X7		
			1 Jan	Balance b/d	1,460
31 Dec	Balance c/d	1,688	31 Dec	Allowance for doubtful debts adjustment	228
		1,688			1,688
20X8			20X8		
31 Dec	Allowance for doubtful debts adjustment	168	1 Jan	Balance b/d	1,688
31 Dec	Balance c/d	1,520			
		1,688			1,688
			20X9		
			1 Jan	Balance b/d	1,520

CHAPTER 9   **Bank reconciliations**

1   (a)   General ledger accounts:

		£	£
Debit	Sales ledger control account	9.00	
Credit	Bank account		9.00

(b)   General ledger accounts:

Debit	Bank charges account	15.80	
Credit	Bank account		15.80

(c)   General ledger accounts:

		£	£
Debit	Gas expense account	300.00	
Credit	Bank account		300.00

(**Note** that if an analysed cash book is used and the postings are made to the general ledger from the totals of the analysis columns at the period end, the above amounts would be included in the totals and posted via the totals.)

2

Cash Receipts Book

Date	Details	£
4 March	J Killick	365.37 ✓
	D Francis	105.48 ✓
5 March	I Oliver	216.57 ✓
6 March	L Canter	104.78
7 March	R Trent	268.59
8 March	P Otter	441.78
		1,502.57

Cash Payments Book

Date	Details	Cheque number	£
4 March	L L Partners	002536	186.90 ✓
	P J Parler	002537	210.55 ✓
5 March	J K Properties	002538	500.00 ✓
	Harmer & Co	002539	104.78 ✓
	Plenith Ltd	002540	60.80
7 March	Wessex & Co	002541	389.40
8 March	Filmer Partners	002542	104.67
			1,557.10

Bank reconciliation statement at 1 March

	£	£
Balance per bank statement		835.68
Less: unpresented cheques		
002530	110.46 ✓	
002534	230.56 ✓	
002535	88.90 ✓	
		(429.92)
		405.76
Add: outstanding lodgement		102.45 ✓
Amended cash book balance		508.21

STATEMENT

first national
30 High Street
Benham
DR4 8TT

SOUTHFIELD ELECTRICAL LTD   **Account number:** 20-26-33 3126897

CHEQUE ACCOUNT   **Sheet 023**

Date		Paid out	Paid in	Balance
1 Mar	Balance b/f			835.68
4 Mar	Cheque No 002534	230.56✓		
	Credit		102.45✓	707.57
5 Mar	DD – National Telephones	145.00		
	Bank charges	7.80		554.77
6 Mar	Cheque No 002530	110.46✓		
	BACS JT Turner		486.20	930.51
7 Mar	Credit		470.85✓	
	Cheque No 002537	210.55✓		
	Cheque No 002536	186.90✓		
	Cheque No 002538	500.00✓		503.91
8 Mar	Cheque No 002535	88.90✓	✓	
	Credit		216.57	
	Cheque No 002539	104.78✓		526.80
8 Mar	Balance c/f			526.80

Bank account

	£		£
Balance b/d (from previous rec)	508.21	Payments	1,557.10
Receipts	1,502.57	Direct debit	145.00
BACS	486.20	Bank charges	7.80
		Balance c/d	787.08
	2,496.98		2,496.98
Balance b/d	787.08		

Bank reconciliation as at 8 March

	£
Balance per bank statement	526.80
Add Outstanding lodgements:	
L Canter	104.78
R Trent	268.59
P Otter	441.78
Total to add:	815.15
Less Unpresented cheques:	
002540	60.80
002541	389.40
002542	104.67
Total to subtract:	554.87
Balance as per cash book	787.08

CHAPTER 10   **Control account reconciliations**

1

Adjustment	Amount £	Debit (✓)	Credit (✓)
Undercast SDB	100	✓	
Sales returns	450		✓
Irrecoverable debt	210		✓

2

Adjustment	Amount £	Debit (✓)	Credit (✓)
PRDB overcast	300		✓
CPB overstated	270		✓
Discount	267	✓	

CHAPTER 11   The trial balance, errors and the suspense account

1

Phone = £3,400 + 300   = £3,700

Insurance = £1,600 – 200   = £1,400

CHAPTER 12   **The extended trial balance**

1   Open up a suspense account to record this difference

2   Both a debit and a credit

3   The closing inventory figure is a $\boxed{\text{credit entry}}$ in the statement of profit or loss columns and a $\boxed{\text{debit entry}}$ in the statement of financial position columns of the ETB.

INDEX

Notes

Notes

Notes

Notes

Notes

REVIEW FORM

How have you used this Text?
(Tick one box only)

☐ Home study

☐ On a course_____

☐ Other _____

During the past six months do you recall seeing/receiving either of the following?
(Tick as many boxes as are relevant)

☐ Our advertisement in Accounting Technician

☐ Our Publishing Catalogue

Why did you decide to purchase this Text? *(Tick one box only)*

☐ Have used BPP Texts in the past

☐ Recommendation by friend/colleague

☐ Recommendation by a college lecturer

☐ Saw advertising

☐ Other _____

Which (if any) aspects of our advertising do you think are useful?
(Tick as many boxes as are relevant)

☐ Prices and publication dates of new editions

☐ Information on Text content

☐ Details of our free online offering

☐ None of the above

Your ratings, comments and suggestions would be appreciated on the following areas of this Text.

	Very useful	Useful	Not useful
Introductory section	☐	☐	☐
Quality of explanations	☐	☐	☐
How it works	☐	☐	☐
Chapter tasks	☐	☐	☐
Chapter overviews	☐	☐	☐
Test your learning	☐	☐	☐
Index	☐	☐	☐

	Excellent	Good	Adequate	Poor
Overall opinion of this Text	☐	☐	☐	☐

Do you intend to continue using BPP Products? ☐ Yes ☐ No

Please note any further comments and suggestions/errors on the reverse of this page. The author of this edition can be e-mailed at: ianblackmore@bpp.com

Please return to: Ian Blackmore, AAT Product Manager, BPP Learning Media Ltd, FREEPOST, London, W12 8AA.

REVIEW FORM (continued)

TELL US WHAT YOU THINK

Please note any further comments and suggestions/errors below

IDEA 15

Spontaneity

Being spontaneous is acting 'on the moment', without pre-planning. Coupling a clear sense of purpose to a tendency to spontaneity offers endless educational opportunities to the children. The famous Japanese poet Matsuo Basho said 'Look children – hailstones. Let's rush out!' And this is an attitude we advocate.

How do you feel about the idea of suddenly bursting into song in your room? Does it fill you with horror, or is such a spontaneous outburst something that you and the children would enjoy? Do you ever notice somebody walking by and wonder to the children where he might be going, then start to make up a story? If you notice a rainbow through the window would you take the children out to look at it? While you're outside, if there are fallen leaves around do you gather them up to use for leaf-printing, pattern-making, picture design or making leaf animals?

Wendy once started singing as one of her children bounced on the trampette. 'Lisa's going up and down, up and down. Lisa's turning round and round, round and round. . .' Lisa grinned, and then she jumped on her knees, forcing Wendy to change the song. Other children wanted a turn, each one trying something different; star-jumping, scissor-legs, varying the rate of the bounce. In this case, the spontaneity of the adult encouraged the same attitude in the children, which was great fun for them, involved them and encouraged creative experimentation – a learning skill that will be of lifelong value.

Your simple *intent* to build spontaneity into your good practice will serve to drive a valuable accumulation of ideas and experiences.

IDEA 16

Do things well enough

'Practice makes perfect.' We have heard people say this many, many times and you probably have too. But how true is it? Perfection means on one level that you could not possibly improve any more, no matter how hard you tried – and indeed, what would be the point of trying anyway? On another level, perfection means that you would be better than everyone else, except those who happened to be perfect too. The idea of perfection is an absolute, so if we say it to children, are we encouraging them towards improvement or setting them an impossible task, with all the attendant pressure that might bring?

At our early years setting we preferred to say 'practice makes better'. This advocates the principle of positive endeavour. We also subscribe to the idea that practice makes *permanence*. Skills and abilities become embedded. But this is a double-edged sword, because bad practice and habit embed themselves just as surely as the good. Guidance and positive encouragement help to embed good practice.

   'I wented to the shops to by some growsaries.'

What was your immediate reaction to that sentence? If a child had written it, would you show him how it should be done correctly? What would you say to him? Would your language include negatives like 'no, not that way' or 'that's wrong'? A corrective approach is one strategy that can be used to help children learn, but we feel it should be supported by the adult's recognition of an *emergent understanding* in the child. Simply put, this means that the child is somewhere along his learning curve: he is learning, and he's getting better through practice. 'Wented' shows a developing understanding of past tense. 'By' indicates ability to match word sound with meaning. 'Growsaries' is phonetically pretty accurate.

Recognizing these positives while encouraging improvement through practice is a powerful strategy for learning.

Winning language – words of encouragement

Sometimes what we see as a failure of capability has its roots in a failure of imagination and/or a failure of nerve. A failure of imagination means that the child has never visualized herself succeeding. It also means very often that the child's habitual mental picture is one of failure. A failure of nerve means that the child is frightened to try in case she fails and perhaps looks foolish in front of her peers and adults.

When working with children there is a lot we can do to address failures of imagination and nerve, to turn them into successes that will have a direct effect on capability.

What if Emily said 'I don't want to draw Mummy because I *can't* draw Mummy!'? What could we say to encourage her? Simply replying 'of course you can' is a denial of how she feels. Just saying 'well, try' suggests effort with no assurance of success. Alternatives that have worked for us include:

- 'Have a go at drawing somebody else. You could make somebody up. Then it doesn't have to look like Mummy.'

- 'Well, pretend you can and let me know when you've finished your drawing.' (This often works very well because 'pretend' makes it safe, because it's no longer 'real', while 'when' presupposes that the child will finish the task.)

- 'Maybe you can't draw Mummy yet. I can't draw my mummy either. Would you help me to try?' (The power of this strategy is that the child's role becomes one of teacher. As she teaches you, she learns for herself. Note also the use of 'yet', which is another presupposition of success.)

What we say can limit or liberate children's progress. Thoughtful use of language encourages – which truly means 'giving them the courage to do'.

IDEA 18

Attainment and achievement

Even at the Foundation Stage, the curriculum is geared towards attainment targets ('stepping-stones') leading towards 'early learning goals'. This occurs largely within a competitive ethos, where children are usually compared against each other and/or some predefined level of competence. Schools themselves are compared in the same way, through 'league tables' and the notion of 'value added' (how much a school has improved compared with its previous performance).

Whether you approve of this model or not, it's surely true that pressure to attain can cause great stress and anxiety in both children and adults. And until the system changes for the better, we have to work within its constraints.

Attainment and achievement are used interchangeably by some people, but we feel that there is an essential difference between them. Remember Emily, who said 'I don't want to draw Mummy because I *can't* draw Mummy!' (Idea 17)? Let's suppose she was sitting next to Mira, who can draw very well indeed for her age. You manage to encourage Emily to have a go. Mira decides to draw too and effortlessly produces a wonderful picture of her mummy in 10 minutes. Meanwhile Emily sits there and tries for 20 minutes. The result is an untidy scrawl.

How do you look upon these two pieces of work?

Undoubtedly Mira's attainment is greater. You could identify many aspects of her work that are superior to Emily's. But whose is the greater achievement? Because of natural talent or greater skill, Mira produced her drawing with little effort, while Emily put in a much greater effort and made something that may well be the best she has done so far. We suggest that Emily's achievement is greater, given that the word means 'to accomplish through endeavour'.

In developing good practice, recognize attainment and celebrate achievement.

IDEA 19

Naming and complimenting

Our names are usually precious to us and form an important part of our identity. To use someone's name immediately creates a powerful link between you. This is an obvious thing to say of course. No less obvious is to greet the children by name as they arrive in your room. This tells them that you have noticed them and acknowledge their presence. It is so much warmer and friendlier than the mechanical registrations they have to endure for the rest of their schooling.

Combining your greeting with a compliment makes the child feel even more special. Wendy would often try to meet new arrivals at the door and typically might say 'Good morning Lucy – oh, I like the dress you're wearing today.' Lucy would feel pleased and often make a point of showing Wendy her shoes as well. Sometimes – just like us – children don't have a good start to the day. Maybe there was a disagreement at home, or perhaps mum or dad was in a bad mood on the journey to playgroup or school. Naming and complimenting is an effective way of changing what could be a negative emotional state in the child. If lots of children are arriving at once, arrange a group gathering where you notice and speak to the children you haven't complimented yet. They will certainly notice if you don't!

However, your praise has to be sincere. False flattery is usually recognized as such and has the opposite effect to what you intended. More broadly, sincerely highlighting the positive is a powerful counterbalance to the often negatively corrective ethos children usually have to cope with throughout their school lives.

IDEA

20

Freedom to choose, explore and imagine

There is a wise old saying in the world of education which goes 'I hear and I forget, I see and I remember, I do and I understand.' Learning by doing is one of the most effective educational strategies that exist. And because children naturally have what has been called *insistent curiosity* they are usually motivated to choose, explore and imagine within the context for learning that you offer them.

Of course, there is not time to allow children to 'rediscover the wheel' in every case. Because the National Curriculum is all about 'coverage', sometimes you simply have to tell the children about things, and in a limited time-frame at that. One effective compromise is to use *the principle of the controlled accident*. This simply means that you set up your session in such a way that children are almost guaranteed to make the discoveries that constitute the learning you want them to have.

One example is when Wendy was doing a session on colour lenses. She had deliberately put out certain colours on the tables and asked the children to 'play' with them – i.e. experiment. It wasn't long before Samantha superimposed a yellow lens over a red one and found that made orange. She was immediately very excited about this and rushed over to tell Wendy, who asked her to show the other children what she had just learned, thus ensuring that Samantha felt proud as well as pleased. And although the other children had not made that discovery for themselves, they saw very clearly how to combine colours to make new ones.

Leonardo da Vinci said that all true knowledge arises from one's own direct experience. Providing those experiences lies at the heart of education.

IDEA
21

Remembering, embedding and ownership

Many years ago the novelist Aldous Huxley wrote an essay pointing out the fragmented nature of the Western educational system, which focuses on the mental accumulation of facts and measures students' success by how many of those facts they can reiterate under formal conditions – that is, how well they can pass exams by recalling the 'right answers'. Nothing seems to have changed in the decades since then.

Other cultures look at learning differently. The scientist F. David Peat (in *Blackfoot Physics**) talks about how Native American peoples view education as a process he describes as 'coming-to-knowing', where understanding is acquired through direct experience and a relationship with the thing to be known. Simply put, it's the difference between trying to explain to a child what salt tastes like and giving him some salt to taste. The power of the learning is in the doing.

Steve remembers sitting in on an ICT lesson once where, for 50 minutes, the teacher talked about computers while all around the children computer screens were blank (as were the faces of many of the children), and not one child got to lay his hands on a keyboard! In contrast to that, at our after-school club 6-year-old Leo showed us things about computers that we never knew before. When we asked him how he had learned all this stuff he said 'Just by playing about to see what happened.' His coming-to-knowing had been very effective indeed.

Repeated direct experience *embeds* knowledge and understanding. It becomes a part of us. The philosopher Michael Polyani calls this *tacit knowledge*. We come to know it not by verbal instruction but by engaging with whatever it is to be mastered. How do we learn to ride a bicycle? And as everybody knows, once you can ride one you never forget how to do it.

* F. David Peal, *Blackfoot Physics* (Newbury Port, MA: Weiser, 2006).

IDEA 22

Self-endeavour and competition

The 'accumulation of facts' model of education usually goes hand-in-hand with an ethos of competition, where predefined standards are imposed upon the learning environment. When children attain these standards they have succeeded, and unfortunately, if they don't attain them, they have not – they have failed. Years ago there used to be the 'ladder' metaphor of attainment. There was the top of the class, the bottom of the class and all the rungs in between. Some teachers would rank children in this crude way based on tests and pin up the list on the noticeboard!

We feel that things have not changed that much. In a world of levels, goals and targets, children are still under pressure to reach a certain rung by a given time in their lives. Children are also often measured one against another, so that no matter how hard Jack tries, if he doesn't reach the same level as Jill he has not done as well.

Sometimes the strategy of competitiveness is useful and positive. In certain contexts, sport for instance, pitting yourself against others can bring out the best in you. The ethos here is not bluntly about winning or losing (though it's often viewed as such), but rather about the achievement of taking part and giving your all. The success is in the trying to improve.

We believe that what links competitiveness in sport with children's learning is the urge to *self-endeavour* – the 'attempt to do', which develops initiative, independence and resilience in the learner.

This idea works well in many ways. We remember Simon, a very angry boy, who through his own endeavours learned to control his temper (most of the time). Sometimes he tried so hard not to have an outburst, and we always praised him for that. Comparing him with Andrew, who was always placid, would have done Simon no good at all.

The fun factor

The psychologist Lev Vygotsky has said that 'The child's greatest achievements are possible in play. Play is the realm of spontaneity and freedom.' Within an educational context we accept that spontaneity and freedom must sometimes (perhaps usually) occur within a planned and structured day. But we also feel that there is a difference between free play – the creative kind of play that leads to exploration and experiment – and an attitude of playfulness or fun. This can happen even in the most prescribed and formal situations.

An attitude of playfulness, what we call 'the fun factor', unites flexibility within a structure, spontaneity and creative improvisation. As with so much else in a learning environment, when you act like this the children know it's fine for them to do so too. In other words, if you see fun in what you're doing, the children are more likely to as well.

For young children particularly, the world is mysterious, wonderful and fresh. Their insistent curiosity drives them to engage with this magical place. Delight and laughter form the natural reaction to their discoveries. As adults we can feed and nurture their sense of fun-in-learning. It is perhaps the most valuable thing we can do for them.

If you are bored when telling a story you've told many times before, then your boredom will make that story (which is new to these particular children) dull and flat. If you are waiting with the children, say, for a bus to arrive to go on a trip, do you help them to notice and question what's around them. If it starts to rain during playtime, do you think or say 'Oh no, not rain again!' Or do you start making up a song about rain and encourage the children to join in?

How far does 'the fun factor' contribute to your good practice?

IDEA 24

A child's-eye view

Young children view the world with a sense of freshness. The essence of their experiences is what the educationalist Margaret Meek has called 'firstness'. Life is naturally marvellous except, alas, for those who learn otherwise. As professionals in the field, part of our task is to appreciate what things look like from a child's-eye view. There are several aspects to this challenge.

Young children don't understand the world as we do. Our perceptions are driven by logic and analysis: we put experiences into neat boxes, whereas for children the irrational and fantastic are often a part of their reality – hence their belief in Father Christmas, the Tooth Fairy and characters in the stories they see and hear. Children will also make up stories to explain what they don't understand. This is an aspect of their development that the educationalist Kieran Egan calls a 'mythic understanding',* which is very different from our grown-up 'sensible' perspective.

The rules and protocols that guide our behaviour may be unknown or unfamiliar to many children. We must teach them these rules with a sense of empathy. If one child snatches something from another, it may be because he doesn't understand the 'etiquette' of the situation. Simple disapproval is not the best way of dealing with it. Patiently explaining why snatching is wrong is a much better strategy. Society is held together by the 'glue' of rules that govern social behaviour. All of these need to be learned.

On a more mundane but no less practical level, the world looks different physically to children. They are 'down there' and we are 'up here'. For them it is filled with giants: us. Have you ever gone down on hands and knees in your room to understand how it looks to a small child? Try it now if no one is looking – or even if they are!

* See Kieran Egan *The Educated Mind: how cognitive tools shape our understanding*. (Chicago, IL, and London: University of Chicago Press, 1997).

Playfulness

Children's natural state is one of play. We don't need to teach them how to do it – but it teaches *them* about rights, rules, roles and responsibilities. It helps them to understand the complex social structure of the world of which they are now a part.

As adults in an early years setting, we must help to ensure that time is made for play. We must also know when to join in with children's play and when it is more appropriate just to let them be. Now and then at playtime in our nursery, the children wanted adults to join in with ball games, chase or hide-and-seek, and on other occasions they just wanted to be left alone. We always respected their wishes either way.

When we do join in with children's play, part of our role can be to help them to extend the game. If children are in the home corner playing mummies and daddies and invite you to play too, you can be a visitor who has come for coffee, or the postman, or the person delivering some groceries. Change and develop the situations so that the children learn a greater repertoire of responses.

Such early play in children, and your attitude of playfulness, will bring further benefits as they move through the educational system, when greater intellectual demands are placed upon them. Success in education (beyond the passing of exams) is most usually recognized in the mastery of knowledge and skills. 'Mastery' in this sense means the ability to manipulate concepts, to recognize insights when they happen and to generate new ideas. The word manipulate suggests an active engagement with those concepts, getting your hands on ideas to take them apart and put them back together again, sometimes in innovative ways. In other words, to play with them.

IDEA 26

Playing safe, staying safe

One important aspect of keeping the children protected is ensuring that your room is as safe as it can possibly be. In a world of rampant risk assessment, we feel common sense and a watchful eye are still your most valuable tools. An occasional 'safety audit' will ensure that precautionary steps you have already taken are still in place and also alert you to possible new sources of danger.

Do the tables have rounded corners? Are cupboards secure against the wall? Have toys and other equipment been tidied away? If you have open shelving, is there anything jutting out that a child could stumble into? If you have vinyl flooring, are mats anti-slip? If you have carpets or mats, are there any small toys, play bricks, etc., underneath? Are there rucks in the matting? Are the windowsills clear? We have known staff leave items such as scissors, spray mount and staple guns on a windowsill intending to put them away later, but in the meantime any child could get his hands on them and hurt himself. If there is anything about the décor or furnishings of the room that you consider to be unsafe, you should, of course, bring this up with the management of the setting.

Another feature of keeping the environment safe is making sure that the children don't get so excited that they are out of control. Developing the knack of exciting them as they learn, but then calming them down when doing what *you* want is largely a matter of experience (also see Idea 51 on Maintaining good behaviour). You must know how to say 'enough is enough' and ensure the children comply. A first effective step is to be 'fully there' for the children. In other words – be aware. Be very aware.

A display board for parents

Having a display board for parents not only allows useful information to be disseminated but adds a welcoming touch that contributes to parents' impression of the setting. If there isn't such a board in your room, perhaps you should suggest setting one up.

At our nursery we made sure that the board was placed where parents could see it and with room to stand and read it. In the vestibule, foyer or cloakroom is ideal. We took time to make sure that the board was kept tidy and up-to-date and that the information was relevant.

Such a board can include notices about local activities, volunteer groups, leaflets about social services, community projects, special events, etc. We also left some empty space for parents themselves to put up information (cot for sale, babysitter wanted or recommended, and so on), plus a suggestions box. Small touches perhaps, but things that have great value in helping the parents to feel included.

'They are what they learn'

We firmly believe that children are born into the world with endless curiosity, a range of natural intelligences and vast potential for growth. What happens to them in the early years creates powerful impressions that are lifelong. The adage 'Give me the child until he is seven and I will give you the man [or woman]' is surely true, although that wisdom is double-edged. The beliefs, values and attitudes that all of us carry as adults, for good or ill, were largely formed in childhood. And although the influence of the home will in most cases outweigh that of playgroup, nursery and school, what we do – what *you* do – every day in an early years setting is going to be important. We are a part of a child's upbringing.

All of us are moulded by our experiences. Quite likely you have friends and acquaintances who can tell stories of how they hated school in general or maths, sport, English, etc., because of the influence of a particular teacher. Confidence can be shattered by an offhand remark. Lack of interest and enthusiasm on an adult's part can 'turn off' that same interest in the child. Ideas poorly explained may remain forever a mystery and a source of frustration. Negative criticism can do immeasurable damage to a child's growing and fragile personality.

As early years professionals, the onus remains on us to create a calm, quiet atmosphere in an organized and stimulating setting. We are most effective in our work when we offer children a range of activities combined with a certain freedom of choice to feed their appetite for new experiences and ideas. Our attentiveness to, and interest in, what they do maintains their courage to explore. Our praise at their achievements will help them to become positive, creative, tolerant adults – which, as Helen Keller said, is the highest aim of any education.

IDEA

29

Food for thought

- A mind once stretched by a new idea cannot return to its original dimensions. (Oliver Wendell Holmes)

- Childhood has its own way of seeing, thinking and feeling and there is nothing more foolish than to try to substitute ours for theirs. (Jean-Jacques Rousseau)

- What we see depends mainly on what we look for. (Sir John Lubbock)

- Be not afraid of growing slowly. Be afraid of standing still. (Chinese proverb)

- Do not confine your children to your own learning for they were born in another time. (Hebrew proverb)

- Even the stone is a teacher. (Idries Shah)

- Having no alternative, we were born creative. (Anon)

- We resent those who take us into deep water when we're still frightened of the shallows. (Hermann Hesse)

- Where is the fun of being a child if you never imagine anything? (Ray Bradbury)

- The most wasted of days is the one without laughter. (e e cummings)

Section 3:
Organization

IDEA 30

Some do's

An organized early years setting is something more than just a neat and tidy place. Organization is one facet of an attitude that maximizes children's opportunities to learn. A systematic approach, attention to detail, regard for the safety and wellbeing of others – these are the hallmarks of good organization and evidence of high standards that are likely to permeate all aspects of your work. In that regard, we hope you find the following tips to be blindingly obvious!

- Keep noticeboards up to date and relevant.

- Check that toys and equipment are in good repair.

- Keep things neat by using clearly labelled plastic storage containers that include a contents list.

- Make sure that jigsaw puzzles, playsets, etc., have all their pieces at the end of each session. This is important, because if a piece is missing it will have just been misplaced and is thus more likely to be found.

- Always be attentive to the safety of the children. Ensure electrical leads are out of the way. Keep instruments and utensils for adult use out of the children's reach.

- Make children aware of any areas that are out of bounds to them (utility room, playground toyshed, etc.).

- If you are working with babies and toddlers keep toys and other things that have been mouthed clean and hygienic using antiseptic wipes.

- Know how many children are in the establishment at all times. If there are several rooms in your setting, someone should be responsible for keeping an up-to-date register. Intercoms in each room are a cheap and effective safety measure.

- Make children aware of procedures and policies. If a student is unfamiliar with parents, guardians, etc., do not let him or her answer the door or allow a child to be collected unless supervised by a staff member.

IDEA 31

And some more do's

Albert Einstein said, 'Keep things as simple as possible, but no simpler.' In an educational world that we feel is overburdened by rules (and in a bureaucratic culture rules beget more rules), it is still important to have clear procedures and policies to help guide the running of any early years setting. And in keeping with Einstein's wise advice, these should be thorough but not overcomplicated. In the final analysis there is no substitute for common sense and a pride in your work – these qualities will lead to the highest possible standards.

It is of course important that every member of staff should not only have read the setting's policy documents but understand them and actively implement them in his or her working practice. Students and new staff members especially need to be clear about this guidance, and the onus is on the headteacher/boss to ensure this is the case. Having said that, responsibility also lies with the employee to *ask* about anything that isn't clear. It is not an admission of failure or weakness to utilize the knowledge of staff. So many problems can be caused by 'raw recruits' who lack experience and the confidence to speak up. The strength of any policy lies in the consistency of its application. The rule, for example, that children mustn't run along the corridors is worthless if a student or new staff member is too shy or lacking in confidence to stop children from running.

At our nursery we used a checklist (see Appendix) as part of an ongoing process of evaluation and feedback. All staff were asked to review their copy regularly and to tick and date (in pencil) their level of understanding and competence in each area. This would be followed by an informal discussion and feedback session where agreement was reached. Boxes would then be initialled and dated.

Arrival time

Our nursery opened at 8.00 a.m., and parents could arrive with their children from that time onwards. Children were registered as they arrived and a running total kept. Such a 'free-flow' system prevented crowding at the front entrance. If crowding ever happened, parents would typically chat with each other while the children grew bored or apprehensive (if they were new to nursery), or ran around becoming overexcited. In fact, for new children, or those we knew were shy or nervous, we would open a few minutes earlier and they would come in first, experiencing a calm and quiet atmosphere before things became busier. It also meant that the cloakroom areas were less clogged and claustrophobic.

We realize that many settings are organized so that all the children are let in at once. In this case, as children and parents gather outside, the provision of tricycles and scooters for children to use means that their time is not being wasted. Similarly, if they have to wait inside, in a lobby area for instance, having crayons and paper handy gives them something useful to do before the day officially begins.

If all children are registered at a specific time each day, a designated member of staff should be there beforehand to chat with them or do singing, rhymes, etc. that can immediately involve them and ensure their time is usefully spent and enjoyable. Meanwhile another staff member can 'meet and greet' arriving parents and deal with any immediate issues and queries. It was always very important to us that the children's day wasn't peppered with 'dead moments', which can be frustrating for everyone.

Waiting times

There are other times when children are in danger of waiting, and, therefore, of wasting their time. At snack times, lunch and playtimes, a system that worked well for us was for the member of staff who was working with the children to let them go down to wash hands, put on coats, etc. a few at a time. This was achieved, for example, by having group singing in which the names of a few children each time were incorporated into the song. When those children heard their names they could leave the room. This made it much easier for another staff member in the toilet area to deal with them as they arrived. It also made sitting at tables in readiness to eat a much calmer affair.

Queuing, we feel, is a particularly irritating kind of waiting. It can easily happen when activities are set up that can only be done by a limited number of children at a time – a painting easel, for instance, with room just for one child, or an art table that might accommodate only four or five. The temptation is for children to hang around until it's their turn. This can disconcert the child who is working and, again, leads to those in the queue being idle.

To get round the problem we had a pot in each room containing the children's names written on card. If a child wanted to do an activity he would find his name-card in the pot and take it to the easel, art table or whatever, place it on a board and then go off and do something else until his turn came around. The cards could be fixed with Blu Tac, velcro or magnets. Alternatively, a staff member might simply write the children's names out on a sheet – although we found that children quite enjoyed having their own 'proper' cards.

IDEA 34

Themes as inspiration

A useful organizational skill is the ability to think both in detail and to 'step back' mentally and have an overview of the work or project in hand. For this reason combining themes and spidergrams works well. Take a large sheet of paper and write the name of your theme or topic in the centre. Brainstorm out from there – in other words, write linked ideas as they come to you around the central theme. Such ideas might be in the form of specific tasks and activities you want the children to undertake and/or include materials you want them to experience. Or, if you have already given these things some thought, earlier or simpler tasks can be placed closer to the centre of the spidergram, while extension or more complex activities can be placed further out. Links with the National Curriculum's Early Learning Goals (ELGs) can be added – using colour-coded dots for the ELGs makes for easier reference and means that the spidergram looks less cluttered.

Tip: As you brainstorm, write your ideas on separate scraps of paper or card so that you can move them around as your thinking and planning evolve.

Opposite is a typical spidergram on the theme of The Jungle. When you have produced your spidergram you might consider putting it up on the wall where the children can see it. Add drawings, pictures and objects to add colour and create visual links to your ideas. This will help the children to 'fix' the relationships between the concepts in their minds and thus serves as a precursor to Mind-Mapping™ techniques.*

Tip: You can't possibly cover everything that appears on your spidergram. Pick the topics that fit in with the time and materials available and keep the other ideas as 'treasures' for the future.

* For more information on mind-mapping™ see, for example, Tony Buzan, *Use Your Head* (London: BBC Books, 1993).

IDEA 35

The value of preparation

We hope you find this concept to be self-evident! Preparation lies at the heart of good practice and makes all the difference between an activity that only goes well and one that goes brilliantly – or between an activity that goes well or disastrously wrong. This point does not contradict the principle of spontaneity (see Idea 15). New good ideas may well come to you more readily as you and the children enjoy an activity that has been carefully thought through and prepared beforehand.

An early stage of preparation involves having an overview of the whole room in which you will be working. Some activities will involve all of the children, but there will be many times when, while you are working with one group, other children will be busy doing different things. Consider where the climbing frame will go, where the art tables will be placed, where an open space might be best sited. Giving early thought to general layout means that the day is more likely to run smoothly and safely.

Carry out such an 'overview visualization' from time to time and consider moving furniture and equipment around. Children like routine, to be sure, but they will also enjoy the freshness of a rearranged room, with new and different things to look at and do.

Once you know where things will go, devote preparation time to individual activities. If you decide to do a lion collage with one group (having created your spidergram earlier – see Idea 34), check what materials you have already and what you need to obtain. This sounds obvious, but so many times we have encountered staff who thought that all they needed was already there in the stock cupboard!

Finally:

- Tackle first tasks you feel confident about.

- Utilize the experience of other staff. Ask, ask, ask!

- Hoard material and other bits and pieces.

- Keep a notebook of ideas.

Collecting ideas

Because of the prescriptive nature of the National Curriculum (a state of affairs that has been with us for many years now) there is perhaps a temptation to do things 'by numbers'. In other words, simply to follow the guidelines or strategies as they have been laid down. The same pressure to 'do it right' might lead practitioners to copy activities they've seen other colleagues do without thinking about adapting or improving them.

We firmly believe that one hallmark of good practice is not just collecting ideas but also developing them creatively. Striving towards this is an ongoing professional challenge that brings a sense of 'ownership' and authentic experience (as opposed to the second-hand experience of always relying on other people's ideas).

A first step is to keep a notebook handy at all times. Anything can spark an idea, which should be written down there and then. Sometimes jottings like this are never developed, but it's more likely that they will form the basis of a fresh approach to things you already do, or even open up entirely new insights that will lead to the development of different and original activities.

As well as a general ideas notebook we recommend that you also collect other resources. Pictures are always useful. These can be cut from magazines and comics, etc. and easily stored in plastic wallets. Alternatively the internet is an endless source of visual material that can be kept on a hard drive or disk.

Elsewhere we have mentioned the value of having a stock of poems, songs and rhymes (see for example Idea 14). These can be organized thematically – for example action rhymes, animal rhymes, name rhymes, (traditional) nursery rhymes, etc. Or smaller topics can be listed alphabetically – beads, cats, dragons and so on.

IDEA 37

Vital pieces of kit

Before we itemize the things that we think are important, consider what you would include in a list of resources that you could use flexibly, that would cover most or all areas of the children's development, that would keep them interested and involved and that incorporate high learning value. Do this before reading on . . .

Our selection would be:

● crayons and pencils, paper, brushes, sponges and paper

● aprons

● at least one string of differently coloured beads for counting and colour recognition

● a container of buttons and beads (different shapes and colours) for threading, counting, sorting and matching

● a numberline (which you and the children could make using the things at the top of the list!)

● favourite books

● a few finger-puppets

● a (themed) anthology of rhymes, songs and poems

● some pictures or photographs incorporating lots of talking-points

● a basket/bag of unusual objects featuring a variety of sizes, shapes, colours and textures

- a CD player with a range of 'world music' and nursery rhyme CDs

- a container of light and flowing 'chiffony' fabrics for music and movement, drama, dressing up, etc.

All of these things would fit into a box that is portable. Feel free to add to our list. And if our choice of any item isn't clear to you, give it some thinking time now.

IDEA

38

Staying fresh

Good practice is about 'staying fresh' and not slipping into routines or sticking with activities that are old favourites, just because that's an easier option. A creative approach to your work requires thought and effort: the effective practitioner is proactive. This often means, as the saying goes, 'moving outside your comfort zone'. Perhaps that phrase is not helpful, because you certainly don't need to feel uncomfortable when trying new things or using all of the resources at your disposal. If you adopt the same attitude of interest, excitement and playfulness you want to cultivate in the children, staying fresh is a delight and not an ordeal or a chore.

A useful first step is to run an inventory of the resources available in your setting. If you are a manager this can be done with all staff, perhaps on a termly basis. Or, as an early years practitioner, you can take the initiative and look closely at what kit you have used or failed to use.

When we ran inventories we found that some staff frequently used the same equipment while other items stayed in the cupboard. There were some pieces of equipment that were never put out by anyone, and thus were being wasted.

Once an inventory throws up observations like this, you can begin to explore the results and the reasons for them. It became clear to us, for instance, that the climbing frame was popular because, once it was put out, certain staff could simply stand back and 'supervise'. Hurdles and hoops were less popular because staff needed to work actively with them and the children for the duration of the activity.

These insights do not need to be seen in a negative light, but as opportunities to maximize resources and the quality of the children's learning experiences.

IDEA

39

Using and valuing outside play space

The outside play space of any early years setting is a valuable resource. Good practitioners know this anyway. When new staff joined our nursery we would tell them that the outside play area should be regarded as an extra room. This was an important point to make, because we have met some staff who think of playtime as a chance to stand with colleagues and chat, while ostensibly 'supervising' the children around them. We even came across one case (at another nursery we hasten to add) when a staff member was sitting sunbathing while the children played nearby!

In fact, outdoor time is a chance to extend the children's play in useful ways – not on every occasion, but sometimes, and as appropriate. If children are cycling, organize a race or a 'cross-country' course. Arrange some cones and have the children weave in and out with their bikes and trikes, or arrange a 'bean-bag pickup'. How might you enrich other activities in this way?

Organized games give children the chance to learn to play them properly through understanding the rules and, just as importantly, to cultivate the qualities of sportsmanship, fairness and integrity in competition. The opportunity also presents itself to address possible gender bias in games. Girls too can play cricket and football and feel just as confident and competent in doing so as the boys.

Displays

Displays form an important part of the children's learning environment. Much of the information that we absorb is visual, so ideally a display will be informative as well as decorative. When planning a wall display, be sure not to clutter or overcrowd the space. As you arrange the items on the display board, position them with drawing-pins (or Blu Tac, though drawing-pins are quicker) and step back from time to time to ensure that each piece is neatly mounted and that the whole display looks balanced. Each child's name should be clearly visible on the work itself or mounted below. When you are satisfied, use a staple gun to fix the pieces permanently. Colourful borders enhance the appearance of any display. A great range of borders with wavy or zigzag edges, or decorated with stars, balloons, etc., is available these days. Some are reversible, with a different colour on each side, and with careful handling can be reused several times. By the same token, don't throw away the backing paper from your old displays; recycle it for painting, collage or cutting-out activities. The overall look of a finished display should be colourful and bold to draw the children's interest again and again.

Consider dedicating one display space for special pieces of work. A 'first-time board' always works well. This features something a child has done for the first time – written his name, cut out a shape with scissors, used red paint in a picture and so on.

Another idea is (with parents' permission) a display of photographs of the children busy with activities during the day.

However, the most important point to be made is that whatever your displays are about, *change them regularly* – at least once a month if time allows. Displays left up for too long become invisible.

IDEA 41

Layout of your room

In the same way that you think ahead when organizing a display (Idea 40), we recommend that you draw a bird's-eye view of your room before setting it up. Represent tables, chairs and large pieces of equipment with bits of card so that you can see how they will look in different configurations (bearing in mind that any arrangement will probably have its advantages and disadvantages). Preparing such a floor-plan takes time, of course, but you only need to create it once and then it becomes a permanent resource that will save you time in the long run.

Something you might consider is using tables as 'partitions' between different areas, but ensure that whatever floor-plan you decide upon the room is not crowded, that there is adequate access to all areas for both the children and yourself, and that safety considerations are always taken into account.

You may decide to arrange your space so that each different aspect of the curriculum has its own discrete area – a play corner, jigsaw table, tables for number apparatus, colour recognition and so on. As children are introduced to concepts and skills in one area, you can then transfer and consolidate them in another. So, if children play counting games at one table and explore colour at another, in the play corner you might ask them to set out four red cups, six blue plates, etc.

Finally – and again, although this takes up valuable time – think about changing the layout of your room from time to time. Although what's convenient for you is important, what's fresh and interesting for the children remains paramount.

IDEA

42

Buying and budgeting for equipment

Since the way that early years settings are financed and funded varies so widely, we can do no more than mention general principles here. But it's certainly true that in this area of developing good practice, common sense can be helped enormously by a 'magpie mentality'. Coupled with your creative attitude, searching out and hoarding equipment and materials isn't about collecting junk but accumulating valuable resources.

An important early decision is whether you intend progressively to improve one area of the curriculum and focus on this, or, on a shorter-term basis, allocate less money in order to fund more areas. One priority for us was gradually to increase our range of musical instruments so that the children had access to a wide variety, some of them unusual and exotic.

If you decide to channel funds into a project like this, be prepared to beg, borrow and – well OK, not steal – other materials you can use. Books can be borrowed from a local library, or bought cheaply from charity shops and jumble sales. The same is true of toys and puzzles. And although it is your time that's being taken up searching these things out, you will save a great amount of money in the process.

When you're building up your stock of dressing-up clothes and materials, ask family, friends and the children's parents if they can help out. We were never too proud to ask parents for old (clean) clothes and pieces of fabric. Most parents were usually only too happy to oblige. We would also pin up requests on our parents' notice board for 'specialist items': if we were arranging a topic on the Chinese New Year we'd ask if any parent had appropriate photographs or objects they could lend us.

Because you will always need to allocate money for 'ongoing materials' like sand, paper, art and craft items, etc., the 'beg and borrow' attitude is bound to serve you well. An added benefit is that it helps parents to feel involved in the life of the early years setting.

IDEA 43

Respect for equipment

The most basic and important point here is to treat equipment as though it were your own. This is but one aspect of taking a pride in your work, which lies at the heart of good practice.

Take time to make sure that your equipment is clean. Children won't want to play with things that are grubby or sticky. If you find for instance that a set of Lego pieces is dirty, arrange a cleaning session that involves the children. Supply them with nail brushes or something similar, protective aprons, and turn what might otherwise have been a chore into 'foamy fun' for the children.

Attentiveness to the condition of equipment in your setting remains a priority. Before deploying dressing-up clothes, take a moment to check for loose threads and if you find some, remove them. They may constitute a danger if they get wrapped around a child's neck or wrist, but even if that risk is slight, clothes and costumes that look ragged or threadbare create a poor impression for visitors.

Be attentive, too, when putting equipment away. It's annoying as well as costly to have to buy a new jigsaw puzzle because one piece has been lost. Turn putting jigsaws away into a counting game with the children. If you have a 100-piece puzzle, ask ten children to count ten pieces each. This has educational value and the children love to feel they've helped.

Make general tidying-up into a game. Say 'Let's see who's fastest, boys or girls (or 3 year olds or 4 year olds, etc.).' If bits and pieces are missing, enlist the children's help by organizing a searching game. Be tactful if you think a child has pocketed an item. Say something like 'Come on everyone, let's check our pockets just in case something's fallen in!'

You never know – this kind of tidying training might turn these children into tidy teenagers!

IDEA
44

Storing and tidying

The fundamental rule here is that everything should have its place. A tidy setting is safer for everyone, it creates a more favourable impression for parents and other visitors, it reflects well on you as a practitioner and it saves no end of time during your busy working day.

Our experience has been that open shelving is most convenient for storage, but if your setting is used by other groups or for different purposes then lockable cupboards are a sensible alternative. We don't recommend using window-sills or other flat surfaces for storage. Not only can this look untidy, but potentially dangerous objects like scissors can so easily be put down inadvertently on a window-sill and create a possible hazard. If you have to store boxes behind other boxes, rotate them on a regular basis, otherwise the equipment kept at the back is much less likely to be used.

Ensure that storage containers are clearly labelled and keep an equipment list in each so that you know what you're looking for when tidying up. If you are taking only some items out of the box – just red things out of a dressing-up box for instance – scribble a quick note to this effect, and that can save time when you're putting things away later.

If items go missing, as they invariably will, make a note of it together with the date. You might find that a pattern emerges, suggesting that a certain child has a 'magpie mentality'. Also, keep a bits-and-pieces box in the staffroom or other suitable place for miscellaneous found items. A new member of staff might not know where things should go and could otherwise leave a small item lying around or put it back in the wrong place. And a central collection pot also saves the embarrassment of having to ask.

Golden rules for time management

- 'Plan the work and work the plan.' In other words, establish a daily routine and keep to it.

- Monitor yourself to discover when you are fresh and alert and when you flag. We all have 'peaks and troughs' of alertness throughout the day – it's called the ultradian rhythm. Attend to the most important matters at the peak times and carry out less significant or onerous tasks when your energies are lower.

- Use deadlines as a 'positive pressure' to complete tasks and stick to them. It's tempting to put off jobs that have open-ended completion times.

- Attend to unpleasant tasks promptly and have done with them. Putting them off means they will only nag away at you.

- Prioritize your tasks. Attend to them in that order. Postpone or forget about things that are actually not necessary.

- Carry out an 'interruptions audit'. What can you do then to avoid interruptions or minimize their effect on your day?

- Insist on 'sacrosanct times' when under no circumstances are you to be disturbed. Be assertive about keeping such times interruption-free.

- Finish what you start and as far as possible work on one task at a time.

- Be organized. Gather your materials, resources, documents, etc. in one place where you can access them easily.

- Arrange specific times for meeting with other staff to discuss routine matters (emergencies are different of course).

- Avoid any tendency towards perfectionism. As the old saying goes, 'perfectionists are never happy'. Do things *adequately.*

- Avoid regretting the things you didn't do. Avoid worrying about the things that you haven't done yet. Get on with the things that have to be done now.

- As far as possible don't take work home with you. Enjoy your evening.

IDEA 46

Classroom management

Good time management and thorough planning build towards effective management of your room and the smoother running of your sessions.

A key factor is being both consistent and insistent as far as the children are concerned. When you have established your own standards and systems in managing the setting, make sure the children know what to do and what you expect of them. Insist on tidiness and be aware that the children can do a lot towards maintaining this. Rather than you tidying up everything, get the children to do it. Cultivate good habits in them of picking up puzzle pieces, building-bricks, etc. for themselves and putting them back in the right place. Obviously this will save you time and effort, but just as importantly it's instilling high standards in the children and helping them to feel that they are contributing in a positive way to making their own learning environment a more pleasant place to be.

Consider also having little boxes and baskets of 'things to do' strategically placed so that children can move on to these if they finish a planned activity before everyone else – paper and crayons, a puzzle, a spirograph set, beads for threading, stencils, building-bricks. These small time-fillers bring diversity into the children's day, and when they know that you expect them to be doing one of these it saves you the trouble of trying to find something for them to do on the spur of the moment.

Finally, always put equipment back where it came from, rather than on the side with the intention of tidying later. And if you've been away for a while, through illness for instance, and someone else has used your room, take time when you return to check that things are where they should be – and put them back if they're not!

IDEA

47

Timetabling tips

Generally speaking, more autonomy – i.e. having your own space and independence – means more flexibility. This usually isn't the case in larger settings with other staff and groups to consider, when, logistically, the easiest course of action is to stick to a more rigid timetable. However, it must always be borne in mind that the timetable is there to serve the children and not the other way around. Its primary purpose is to bring variety and diversity into the children's day; it should not be an inflexible structure to which everything else is subservient.

We make this point because, even in the early years, there may be a pressure to 'cover ground' in order to satisfy the Early Learning Goals. Many years ago the psychologist Howard Gardner asserted that 'coverage is the enemy of understanding'. This is no less true today. However, if the timetable in your setting allows for some flexibility (and if it doesn't, you might like to investigate ways of rectifying this) and if you bring a creative attitude to your practice, then coverage *per se* becomes less of a problem.

Practically speaking, your creative attitude sees everything as a resource and an opportunity. If there is a rain shower that prohibits outside play, stretch the current session or organize another activity, perhaps something you haven't run for months, which will delight the children. If the rain produces a rainbow, 'think spontaneous' (see Idea 15) and think how you can utilize this moment educationally. Do you know any rainbow songs, rhymes or stories? Can you slot in a bead-threading activity so that the children can create rainbow necklaces? (You'll need to know your stock and equipment in this case.)

Play your part in ensuring that the timetable is a structure that supports rather than a cage that imprisons.

IDEA 48

Record-keeping

Our advice is to keep it short and sweet. It is our belief that the mentality that is a slave to coverage (see Idea 47) also feels the need to maintain endless records at the expense of interacting with the children. Apart from being a wasted opportunity to help children learn, sitting beside a child and making notes evokes what is called the 'observer effect'. This can be a real problem. The fact is that the child will know that you're making not just observations but also judgements about him. This can have a detrimental effect, changing the child's behaviour and draining his confidence. If you can avoid this situation, do so at every opportunity.

Of course many settings already have a record-keeping system set up. If so, is it unobtrusive, efficient and accurate? If not, perhaps you might want to suggest a better alternative. We used a simple 1–3 number system:

1   Has mastered a skill to the point where s/he usually achieves success.

2   Has some capability with the need for minimum supervision.

3   Skill is being introduced and child has little or no experience. Supervision and guidance needed.

This simple scale can be used in conjunction with the Early Learning Goals and/or your own checklist of skills and activities. And rather than using a tick or cross, we would put the date of the observation in the appropriate box, or with appropriate number beside the skill being assessed. This is because children soon come to understand ticks and crosses – and indeed will be exposed to them throughout their educational career.

Our imperative is always to minimize the time spent writing up notes and maximize the time we could be interacting with the children.

Even if you find that such a strategy won't work at the 'summative assessment' stage of a child's progress, try using it on a week-by-week basis as you form more detailed impressions.

IDEA

49

Fire procedures

We take it as given that there is an established fire procedure at your setting. However, one possible problem (and a weakness in the system) is that if fire-drills are carried out regularly on the same day of the week, or worse, at the same time then (a) children who don't attend on that day will not be familiar with the procedure and (b) children (and staff) who are always there for fire-drill can become complacent. Another problem occurs if drills are carried out too infrequently: we have come across settings that run them only once a term.

The point is that fire procedure should not be regarded as an inconvenience and a chore, but rather as a vital aspect of the setting's safety and, as with everything else that goes on there, an opportunity for the children to learn.

Our strategy was to have a fire-drill at least once a month. Because of the size of our setting we ran on a six-month cycle. The months of the year were written out on scraps of paper, with each month written twice. Each staff member drew out two scraps. These would be the months when that person organized a fire-drill. This is a double-blind system where no one else, not even the team-leader, knew who was organizing any drill, or when it would happen.

We found that this more realistic simulation overcame the problems mentioned above and generally kept both children and staff on their toes. The frequency of the drills meant that everyone got used to keeping calm during these unexpected situations. Do you find this rather too complicated and troublesome? Not when you consider that one day the fire might be real.

IDEA 50

Assertiveness and direct positive action

Many of the ideas mentioned in this book, and the whole underpinning aim of developing good practice, depends upon the attitude you bring to your work. Professionalism is more than a matter of paper qualifications or even 'length of service'. Having done the job for a long time and being an experienced early years practitioner do not necessarily amount to the same thing.

We feel that a vitally important aspect of one's professional attitude hinges on assertiveness and the willingness to take direct positive action where necessary.

Assertiveness is not the same as being overconfident, arrogant or aggressive. While being assertive aids self-confidence, it is the opposite of cockiness and aggressiveness (which tend to be defences masking vulnerability and weakness).

Some of your basic assertive rights are

- To make your own decisions, take your own actions and reflect upon their possible consequences.

- To make mistakes as you learn and to realize that you *can* learn from them.

- To say 'I don't know/understand.'*

Becoming more assertive is often a matter of taking direct positive action. Reflect now on times when you have acted in this way and the benefits that resulted from it. Conversely, think back to times when you were negative in your thinking or indecisive in action, and the problems that caused. What situations might arise in your work where direct positive action would probably improve matters?

Wherever you are in your career, remembering your basic assertive rights and taking direct positive action in dealing with things not only helps you but, as always, creates the opportunity for children to mimic and learn from your behaviour.

* To learn more about assertiveness we recommend Manuel J. Smith's book *When I Say No, I Feel Guilty* (New York: Bantam Books, 1975).

Section 4:
Social Development

IDEA 51

Maintaining good behaviour

We mean, of course, maintaining good behaviour in the children! Your attitude of assertiveness and your willingness to take direct positive action (see Idea 50) will be invaluable here – as will consistency in the way you act.

A powerful and important strategy you can employ is 'Ask, Tell, Do'. If a child is doing something you disapprove of, ask him (or her) to stop. To do this, say the child's name first, then establish eye-contact and make sure the child keeps looking at you so that you know he is listening to what you say. Ask the child to stop doing whatever it is you disapprove of. But frame the question carefully. Saying 'Would you like to pick up that piece of litter now?' hands control to the child and creates the opportunity for him to say 'No'. Beware also of rhetorical questions such as 'Do you expect me to stand here and wait for you to pick up that litter?' This can so easily sound sarcastic, and sarcasm is never the mark of the professional.

Instead, say in a firm tone, 'Will you pick up that litter now please?' Be polite, firm – assertive. Don't walk away expecting the task to be carried out. Wait, and then if the child says 'No' or doesn't respond, say 'I've asked you nicely to pick up the litter. Now I'm telling you to do it.' If this still doesn't get the result you want, physically intervene. Take the child's hand and take it to the litter, even if it's you that picks it up. Walk the child over to the bin and put the litter in. This version of direct positive action often results in children agreeing to do it by themselves if, for instance, someone has deliberately dropped a jigsaw puzzle on the floor.

Note: If children are being aggressive to one another, you must of course intervene physically at the outset.

Treat others as you would wish to be treated

IDEA 52

We make the point again here, as we have in other Ideas, that this aspect of your professional attitude not only benefits you and the adults you deal with in your work but shows the children what such an attitude looks like and sounds like. In other words, it gives them a type of behaviour to mimic and learn from. Indeed, actively cultivating this attitude in them equips them with a vital social skill that will bring benefits throughout their lives.

A very important thing for children to learn is empathy – seeing the world from someone else's perspective. When a child can do this she (or he) can much more easily treat others as she would like to be treated.

At our nursery if one child hit another we would say to the aggressor 'How do you think [the victim] feels? You wouldn't like him to do that to you, would you?'

Often this is enough to foster understanding and bring an apology. Sometimes, though, the strategy can surprise you. On one occasion a boy had hit another boy and we used the ploy of 'That wasn't a very nice thing to do. How would you feel if it was done to you?' The aggressor shrugged and said, 'I don't care, it wouldn't hurt' – whereupon the victim thumped him hard, and he cried. This wasn't something we'd intended, but the point had been made very directly and, interestingly, those two little boys became quite close friends after that.

Criticize the behaviour, not the child

Consider the difference between saying 'Don't do that. You are such an unkind child!' and 'I think that was a really unkind thing to do!' We hope the difference is not only obvious to you but also a matter of concern. In the first instance the child herself is being labelled as unkind – a judgement is being made about the child's very character. In the second instance that particular piece of behaviour is being criticized.

In psychological terms to say that someone *is* unkind (or some other label) is to create a 'nominalization' – think of it as a 'name-inalization'. Imagine a label with that name on it hanging around the person's neck. It encourages a mental state. And a state is static, and something static can be stuck. On the other hand, with this in mind, behaviour is regarded as a process, which implies movement and change. 'To process', as a verb, means to move forward. So commenting on the behaviour emphasizes actions that can be changed.

As an exercise, next time you visit the supermarket notice how parents speak to their children. Be aware of how often the children themselves are negatively criticized rather than the behaviour they are engaging in at that moment. And notice how often adults nominalize themselves by saying things like, 'I'm useless', 'I'm hopeless', 'I know it's stupid of me to say this but ...' And so on.

Our belief is that a person's self-esteem should truly be how we estimate ourselves – it's *self*-esteem. Whereas, ironically, some people's view of themselves is often influenced or even largely determined by others' opinions of them. Help children to develop higher self-esteem by avoiding damaging labels and by giving them the chance to correct inappropriate behaviours.

Cooperation and sharing

This point has popped up in a number of other ideas in this book because it is of such great importance. At our nursery we had three rules we wanted all staff to abide by:

- No individual may harm or hurt another individual.

- If a person is working on something you want to work on, you must wait your turn and not interrupt their work.

- Whatever you work on, leave things as you found them.

You may think these are naïvely obvious things to say and might even feel patronized that we mention them, but our experience occasionally was that even staff members with years of service would 'forget' these rules and sometimes, alas, deliberately disregard them.

Another crucial aspect of this issue involves sharing concerns and grievances. If staff members did not get on well together we encouraged them to air the matter and not let things simmer unspoken, and certainly not lead to sniping and gossip. Our 'social filters' are often invisible to us and it is so easy to judge and discriminate (positively as well as negatively) without realizing it. If our concerns are brought into the open they can more easily be resolved.

Of course, developments in our own self-awareness in this regard will have a positive effect on the children. But there are things you can do more explicitly to foster cooperation, sharing and mutual understanding. For example

- We would explain to the other children why 'special needs' children at nursery were unable to do certain things or did things differently.

- We let children of different ages mix and work together.

- We would let 'normally sighted' children try on spectacles to gain insights (as it were) into the needs of children who had to wear glasses.

Take time to add to this important list.

IDEA 55

Mixed age groups

At our nursery we practised a 'free-flow' system, where children of different ages could mix and work together. We realize this may not be possible in many settings, but the strategy has great advantages if you can implement it even in a limited way.

Our belief is that mixed age groups in each room is closer to the home experience, where older children have the opportunity to see the younger ones develop. Older children come to understand that there are things they can do that the younger ones can't. This realization often fosters helpfulness in them. By the same token, the younger children can mimic the more sophisticated behaviours and skills of the older ones and in some cases this accelerates their own development.

Free flow also highlights the whole issue of labelling and compartmentalizing people (see Idea 53). We feel that children will experience enough of this (too much of it actually) in their schooling. Interacting with other individuals and appreciating people for who they are is what counts, free of the limiting effects of categorizing them.

IDEA 56

Relaxation and calming

Dr Herbert Benson in *The Relaxation Response** asserts that our ability to relax and be calm is as natural and powerful as the 'fight or flight' response that's familiar to most people. Even so, the capacity to relax quickly and effectively needs to be cultivated – and where better to start this training than with young children?

Build 'calm times' into the day. Make them part of the routine. Explain to the children that these quiet times are for being settled and still. Have soothing mood music playing in the room. Show children how to slow and deepen their breathing. This is an ancient and powerful way of achieving a profound state of tranquillity. Demonstrate slow bends and stretches (nothing strenuous) that will help children to get rid of physical tension. Try similar breathing and movement activities with the children lying on the floor. Then ask the children simply to lie quite still and to notice how good that feels. Ask them to imagine moving their fingers *without actually moving them*. This focuses the attention and takes the children's minds off distracting or worrying thoughts. During our relaxation times we'd also ask the children to put a chiffon scarf over their eyes. The touch of the material was itself soothing, but it also acted to 'still the view' as the children looked through it.

During these times and throughout the day, notice how you use your voice and manner. When you are calm and your voice has a soothing tone the children will respond accordingly.

* Herbert Benson, *The Relaxation Response* (New York: William Morrow, 1975).

Dealing with emotions – some quick tips

This is a huge topic and advice is abundant and easily available. Ideas that we have found useful include:

- Negative emotions that cause tearfulness, clinginess and tantrums happen for a reason. Don't assume simple 'naughtiness'. Be prepared to explore the context of the emotion with the child.

- Help a child to control and 'rein in' anger or upset by working on calming the breathing (see Idea 56). Have a quiet area where a child can go to settle down and perhaps talk with a favourite staff member (who may not be the child's key worker).

- If you want to deal with the situation within your own room, remember the Ask, Tell, Do strategy (Idea 51). Gain the child's attention and tell him what he is doing that you find unacceptable. Ask him to stop and make it clear what the consequences will be if he doesn't. If he doesn't stop, carry out the action/strategy you've decided upon to deal with the situation (making him sit in a 'time out' area, for instance).

- Be clear, firm and consistent – not only in dealing with outbursts but also in your general instructions to the children. They can become overwhelmed by too many things to remember and do.

- In the case of temper tantrums, do not get into an argument or a battle. Do not give the child control of the situation. And don't try to shout above the child's crying or screaming. We found that sometimes the shrill blast of a whistle worked very well in restoring order by shocking the child out of his behaviour.

- Of course, as you get to know your children, you'll discover what can 'set them off' and perhaps take steps to avoid those situations.

- In all cases talk to the parents about the incident at the first opportunity.

IDEA 58

Emotional release

The American psychologist Howard Gardner has suggested that people are intelligent in many ways. He includes in his repertoire of intelligences the notion of 'emotional intelligence' – our ability to be aware, knowing, understanding and capable of modifying emotions in ourselves and others.

Emotional intelligence (EI) is a potential we all possess, but fulfilling it does not tend to happen by accident. EI needs to be developed and cultivated as part of a child's general learning. Becoming emotionally intelligent needs to be part of a child's education.

One activity we did with the children at nursery allowed them to experience what different emotions looked like, sounded like and felt like. We would play the 'pretend to yawn game', then ask them to pretend to cry, to laugh (a 'giggle bag' works really well here). We'd ask the children to stamp their feet, pretend to be angry, rub hands together in a temper. Of course, although it was only pretend the activity began to evoke the emotions for real. As emotions rose we'd get the children to change them, from anger to laughter for instance.

The lesson here is that children become more aware of how emotions appear and grow, and realize they can often choose to change a feeling, release it harmlessly or 'switch it off'.

If you use this activity, be aware of children who don't like it or can't cope with it. It's also important that you know you have the confidence to 'bring things back to normal' when you choose.

IDEA 59

Managing children's behaviour

As with other topics we've explored in this book, behaviour management is a huge issue and there is a vast amount of guidance available. In terms of basics:

- Know the context in which the behaviour occurs. Obviously if a situation is unfolding quickly you have to step in and deal with it. But sometimes it's wiser to stand back, count to ten and then step in to intervene calmly.

- Be aware of your own emotional state. When you intervene, don't get tangled up emotionally yourself. Remain detached and in control. It's also true that your emotions communicate themselves 'non-verbally' to the children. If you're tense they'll pick up on it. If you're calm, that influences them too.

- You will, of course, need to follow the behaviour management guidelines in place at your setting, but be aware that some sanctions will work better with certain children than with others. Be flexible in applying the rules.

- New children won't know the rules, the routines and the people at the establishment. Their nervousness and uncertainty can lead to what might easily be interpreted as bad behaviour.

- Help to cultivate an atmosphere of calmness, respect, understanding and supportiveness. The 'ambience' of the setting will have a powerful effect on how the children behave.

IDEA 60

Maintaining good behaviour

In our view maintaining good behaviour amongst the children is a matter of being *firm*, *fair* and *consistent*. Firmness means that once you have agreed the standards of conduct that you want (either in your own mind or as a matter of policy at the early years setting) you insist that the standard is kept, using whatever strategies work best for you. Firmness also means that you must be prepared to carry out what you have said you will do. If you have told a child that if she throws a toy once more you will take it away from her, if she throws it again you must do this.

Perhaps you are not only thinking that this is an obvious thing to say but also 'Well, of course I'd take it off her!' Maybe you would, but we have seen many, many instances when parents and early years practitioners have threatened to carry out a punishment and then not done so. Why? Possibly because the parent doesn't want to be embarrassed by the child's temper tantrum, or perhaps the child is one of the practitioner's favourites. Whatever the reason, not following through with your action isn't good for you or for the child.

Similarly, when you have told the child to stop doing something you disapprove of, don't just turn away and let the child carry on doing it. Use your presence, including eye-contact, facial expression and the tone of your voice as part of your insistence that your instruction is carried out. By 'tone of voice' we do not mean shouting. Shouting (whether you actually lose your temper or not) is the start of the slippery slope to falling standards. Raise your voice sparingly and it will have far more impact when you do so.

IDEA
61

Bullying issues

Bullying takes many different forms along a covert–overt spectrum. Bullying is also knowing and systematic. We feel that bullies may not know *why* they are being like that, but they know that they *are* being like that. Even something as subtle as a child deliberately ignoring another over time counts as bullying. So we as adults and 'caring presences' need to be watchful and ready to act.

The calm supportive atmosphere we mentioned in Idea 59 will help to dampen instances of bullying. In addition to this, if a child starts nursery who is different in some way from others, we would explain why to all concerned: 'Although Sarah's 4 she can't walk yet because the muscles in her legs aren't working properly.' Cultivating understanding acts against the unthinking prejudice that often motivates bullying.

We would also encourage the children to bring instances of bullying out into the open: in other words, to tell somebody. This is obvious common sense. Bullying thrives in secret. When children tell an adult what's going on, not only will you most likely have the right strategy to deal with it, but the child's own display of confidence is a positive breakthrough.

Section 5:
Skills for Learning

Observational skills

Although at first glance 'observational skills' might be taken to refer to what children see, we would like the idea to encompass all of the senses, and we will reflect on this below and in Idea 63.

It is also telling that we use the term 'skills', which implies that children have the *potential* to observe with increasing discrimination and subtlety, but that potential must be developed by sustained and progressive programmes of activities. A common strategy is to work towards children doing representational drawings – obviously to copy something they have to observe it carefully. Start, perhaps, with a straight line, a horizontal one first, then a vertical one. Move on to a circle, a square, a triangle, though be aware that some children as old as 5 find these more complex shapes difficult.

Representational drawing is, of course, a matter of physical coordination as well as observational acuity. Another factor might be what we call *failure of nerve*. Here, children are capable of the task but are frightened to try because they think they'll fail or that the result won't be good enough. Gentle encouragement and choosing your words carefully can work well here, as will a careful progression towards the more sophisticated tasks you're aiming for.

When asking children to draw, for instance, a vase of flowers, ask for a 'blob painting' first to capture general shape and colour. Afterwards draw children's attention to petals, stamens, leaves, stalks and so on.

Take every opportunity to develop observational skills. Think of how many activities through the day where this can be achieved.

IDEA

63

Developing sensory acuity

All of our senses are linked. One outcome of developing observational, auditory and tactile acuity (to name a few) is to enrich children's overall experience of the world. Here are a few tips to get started:

- Collect a boxful of natural objects: stones, shells, seeds, feathers. Have children handle these and talk about what they see and feel. Build on this with a 'feelie box' of items of varied shapes, sizes and textures.

- Have a 'smell session'. Sometimes children like to wear a blindfold as they smell, for instance, peppermint, a tangerine, a jelly-baby, a fresh piece of banana. Often children's responses will be to guess at the thing being smelt, but try to encourage them to talk about the smell itself. Instead of 'tangerine' strive for 'tangy, a bit sweet, fresh', etc.

- Run a tasting session. We found that asking children (again with eyes closed or blindfolded) to notice the difference in taste between black grapes and green grapes worked well. Also try pieces of green, yellow, orange and red peppers cut to similar size. It's healthy too!

- For sounds, have the children sit or lie very still and ask them to listen out for tiny sounds. We also showed our children what different musical instruments sounded like and then played them behind our backs for the children to guess the instrument and/or talk about the sound itself.

IDEA
64

Concentration

Concentration is also a skill (see Ideas 62 and 63), one of sustained attention on external events and/or internal mental impressions. Developing this skill early will bring great benefits throughout a child's educational career.

Interest encourages concentration. When a child is interested in what's going on then deeper and more sustained involvement naturally follows. Intense involvement in the object of concentration is called *immersion*, and is a key factor in a child drawing the richest experience and the greatest learning value from a task.

What can we, as early years practitioners, do to cultivate the skill of concentration?

● Exploit children's natural curiosity by showing and telling them things that will fascinate them. If you find an interesting leaf, seed or insect, bring it in and show it to the children.

● Develop your storytelling skills (see our book *100 Ideas for Teaching Creative Development**). Your 'storytelling voice' can either be monotonous and uninteresting, or full of wonder, variety and subtlety of tone.

● Do a 'whisper session' where you say things very quietly so that the children have to listen hard.

● Contrast 'ambient awareness' with focused concentration. Let children listen to all the sounds coming from, say, the next room or from outside. Then get them to concentrate on just one sound. Let their eyes absorb an entire painting, then draw their attention to tiny details.

* Wendy and Stephen Bowkett, *100 Ideas for Teaching Creative Development* (London: Continuum, 2008).

Display boards and interest tables

We've already touched upon the usefulness of display boards in Idea 40. Obviously they have value while you are working on a theme or topic with the children. The visual presentation of information aids learning greatly. Children glance at, and are exposed to, those ideas many times through the day, and of course you can deliberately draw their attention to what is on the boards, which act as a focal point for discussion and enquiry. A colourful display stimulates interest and also literally shows parents and other visitors what the children are currently engaged in.

But you might also consider using a display board dedicated for a week or so to a single child's work, making him or her feel special and creating the opportunity to show enthusiasm about a hobby or a recently completed drawing. If you have a large group which makes weekly individual displays difficult, dedicate a display to children whose names begin with the same letter, or who share a birthday month. Individualizing displays in this way boosts confidence and self-esteem.

Display boards and interest tables might also be used to display examples of a new technique that the children have learned. If a child returns from holiday with their hair braided for example, the board or table could include beads for threading and braiding for older children plus information about the technique and its history. This links the requirements of the National Curriculum with the children's own experience and thus creates relevance for them.

Drawing out the language

Language development is a huge topic and is, of course, central to the success of any child's education. The word 'education' means 'to draw out and rear up' (from the Latin *educatio* and *(e)ducere*). A basic principle to bear in mind, therefore, is to draw out the children's language whenever possible, with the aim in mind of helping them to be independent, confident and creative in its use. A couple of tips that we think important are:

- Build children's vocabularies by adding to what they have said. If Daniel shows you his nice new blue jumper, comment on it with, 'Yes, that looks like a lovely warm, fluffy blue jumper.' Create opportunities for children to hear a range of relevant adjectives, verbs and adverbs in the natural context of everyday conversation. A great deal of learning occurs by osmosis, which is to say that children absorb knowledge and ideas without necessarily understanding the rules behind the process.

- Ask open questions that call for a more extended and elaborate response from the children. If Lucy says, 'I went to my Auntie's on Saturday', there is limited value in responding with, 'Did you?' or 'Oh, you went to your Auntie's on Saturday!' More usefully, you can ask Lucy what she did at her Auntie's or what Auntie's house and garden are like. Think about how you can keep a conversation going. This makes a child feel special, it teaches the conventions of day-to-day language and it develops attention and concentration.

IDEA 67

Manipulation of tools and equipment

Everything that goes on in your room is a learning opportunity for the children. If you have not done so yet, stand back and think about how children handle the implements and equipment that form part of their day-to-day routines. Children need to be told the important do's and don'ts of this. Tell them to hold a pair of scissors by the closed blades. Similarly with pencils – hold point downward. Tell children not to put pencils or other implements in their mouths, ears or noses. If a child must carry a chair, tell him to hold it with the chair-back against his arm, not against his chest. In the latter case, if he stumbles the chair-back can strike up into his throat. Try in any case to minimize the carrying of implements and furniture.

Search for the best or most useful versions of equipment available. Do you have left-handers in your group? Left-handed scissors and other implements are readily available these days. Consider buying triangular rather than round or hexagonal pencils. Triangular pencils help children to learn the proper 'pencil grip' much more effectively.

In summary, be alert to safety and effectiveness in this aspect of your good practice.

IDEA 68

Hand–eye coordination

Education is about fulfilling potential. Although arguably most, if not all, children will develop a degree of hand–eye coordination anyway, this skill can be 'brought on' more effectively and quickly by the considered provisions of your setting and by deliberately building appropriate activities into the children's day.

Essential items, therefore, are crayons and pencils (triangular as appropriate – see Idea 67), inset puzzles, pegboards, threading-boards, posting boxes and the like. Further develop hand–eye coordination through simple physical activities. With the children sitting on the floor, ask them to touch a finger of one hand to the opposite knee, or an elbow to the opposite knee. With children standing, get them to do toe-touches, right hand to left foot and vice versa. Increase the fun factor and the learning value by practising finger-rhymes such as Tommy Thumb or 'One finger one thumb, keep moving' (see our book *100 Ideas for Teaching Creative Development* for more information).

Very powerful techniques for developing hand–eye coordination can be found in the field of *educational kinesiology* (also known as Brain Gym®), which explores and exploits the relationship between brain development and specific learning tasks. Much pioneering work has been done by Paul and Gail Dennison, who have helped to bring 'Edu-K' to a wide audience. Their simple techniques are based on the proposed principle that when limbs cross the mid-line of the body, neural connections are stimulated and strengthened between the right and left cerebral hemispheres of the brain.*

* For more information on this fascinating subject contact the Educational Kinesiology (UK) Foundation (www.braingym.org.uk) and related books published by Edu-Kinesthestics Inc of California (www.braingym.com).

IDEA 69

Bead and button box

We learn by 'using all of ourselves'. Understanding happens through our physical and sensual experience at least as much as it does through our thinking, remembering and imagination. Something as simple and inexpensive as a bead and button box highlights the point.

For previous generations of children, a box of buttons and beads was a familiar sight around the house. And how fascinating and pleasurable it was (if you were allowed!) to push your hands into it and feel those tiny objects slipping through your fingers and hear all the little sounds they made.

For little money and effort you can give that experience to all of the children in your setting. Buttons and beads can be bought very cheaply at charity shops and bric-à-brac stalls, although 'specialist' big buttons can be obtained through educational suppliers. The advantage of these is mainly that children can't swallow them, put them up noses or in ears, etc. If you opt for common-or-garden buttons and beads you can thread them for safety reasons, but this denies the children the opportunity of using them for counting, matching, pattern-making, comparing, measuring, grading, threading – and letting them slip through their fingers. Closely supervise children during all of these activities.

IDEA 70

Number through rhyme and story

We remember a little boy at our nursery who began counting with the number 2. He did not have any idea about number 1. The reason, we discovered, was that previously when an adult did counting with him she would start him off by saying (for instance) 'Let's count these buttons. One...' and he would continue with 'two, three, four...'

This illustrates an extremely important point. There is a difference between children's ability to count and their understanding of the *concept* of number – or, as we prefer to say, their 'sense' of number. Can a child apply the concept of, say, 'five' to his everyday experience? That is a vital measure of his understanding.

By the same token, conceptual understanding can be developed *through* everyday experience, and there is no better way than by using rhyme and story. Begin by collecting examples: create your own anthology. When you do these with the children, get them physically involved. If you do 'Five currant buns in the baker's shop', choose five children to be the buns. As each is picked in turn, those children physically move away. *They are the numbers.* A friend of ours always teaches number, albeit to older children, in this way. Isaac Anoom (aka Mr Numbervator) supplies the group with numbered T-shirts and teaches arithmetic and algebra by having the children literally arranging and rearranging themselves to make 'living equations'.

The same kind of creativity can inform your own good practice. Instead of the Three Little Pigs, do the story of the Five Little Pigs and get the children to help you decide on what else the pigs can use to build their houses and what big bad wolf gets up to. Not only does this put more fun into the activity, but it helps children to explore and boost their own creative abilities.

IDEA 71

Sorting

Sorting is a skill that children tend to develop in an 'organic' way through their play. Notice that when a group of children play with a farmyard set, they'll put the hens in the hen-pen, the sheep in one field and the cows in another. If this is happening anyway there is perhaps no need to intervene, although there may be occasions when you'll want to encourage it. Similarly, if a group is playing with toy cars you can suggest that the red cars can be parked in the garage while the green cars take the children to the park and the blue cars go to the shops, etc.

It's important, of course, that the toys and other resources in the setting lend themselves to sorting games, but in any case your own inventiveness will play a part. When the children are using building-bricks, for instance, you can set them tasks such as separating out bricks of the same size and colour, or ask for a blue door, two red windows and two green ones, one white wall and so on.

Sorting skills can be as simple or as complex as you feel they need to be to suit the current capabilities of any child. But in all cases they act as precursors to more sophisticated kinds of thinking such as sequencing, attributing, categorizing and classifying. For more detail on this see for example, *100+ Ideas for Teaching Thinking Skills*.

* Stephen Bowkett, *100+ Ideas for Teaching Thinking Skills* (London: Continuum, 2007).

IDEA 72

The value of games

We have found that using card, board and other games is a lovely way of working with small groups. An immediate benefit is that you can monitor a range of tasks and skills for each child unobtrusively, without the necessity of ticksheets and other paperwork. It's important, however, that you join in the game and be involved as one of the players. Sitting apart and watching can inhibit the children, especially if you interrupt their play with comments and suggestions. Besides, that's not as much fun for you!

Favourite games in our setting included dominoes, Snap, Happy Families, Twister, Pick-a-Stick, Tumbling Monkeys and games featuring colour and number dice. As with the sorting activities mentioned in the previous idea, such games allow children to learn as they play in a natural and organic way. Building games into your sessions develops children's language, listening and communication, and fine motor skills, as well as important social qualities such as waiting their turn, sharing and cooperation, complying with agreed rules and so on. Further value rests in the development of children's conceptual understanding and their perception of things.

Even though most games are quite formal, you can still use your creativity to extend them, by singing number rhymes while playing dominoes for instance, or reciting colour poems during Ludo, or improvising monkey rhymes as you play Tumbling Monkeys. Another way of drawing the greatest value from games is not just to talk about the rules with the children, but to think about how games can be altered and extended by adding to or changing the rules.

IDEA 73

Recognizing effective learning

At the heart of the matter, we feel that children will learn effectively when they are happy, settled and involved. And in order for them to feel this, we think that you should be too. Your own sense of enjoyment and fulfilment through creative engagement in what you do will have a powerful and pervasive effect on every child who comes to your setting. This is, of course, not something that can be legislated for, imposed, insisted upon or forced. It is a quality that only you can bring to your good practice and one that will resonate with the children who, especially at that early age, are naturally curious, playful and enthusiastic.

Our firm belief is that the primary purpose of education is to cultivate these natural human attributes and predispositions and use them as the motivating force in the development of all the other skills and abilities the children will need to be creative, independent thinkers and tolerant, understanding human beings.

There is a Jesuit saying, 'Give me the boy until he is 7 and I will give you the man.' We think this as true today as it ever was. Early influences have a lifelong effect and one of the most important for the children who come to your setting is you.

Section 6:
Imagination and Play

Some relevant questions

Play has great educational value. Because it is not, and should not be considered as, a time-filling frivolity, we think it's important to reflect on the following questions:

- Are the play activities you choose meeting the needs of all of the children (having, of course, previously identified those needs)?

- Do the activities stimulate interest and involvement?

- Can you develop at least some of the activities to include and extend more aspects of learning or the Early Learning Goals?

- Do the children have enough time to finish an activity you've planned?

- Do the children realize they have a certain time in which to finish the activities they start?

- Will there be an opportunity for children to finish an activity they've started once the session itself is over? (Sometimes children really do need to complete it for their own satisfaction and peace of mind.)

- Do the children know what you've planned through the day? In other words, do they have a sense of time and progression? Such understanding helps them to anticipate and look forward to the activities.

- Do you as an adult have the opportunity to join in and share the children's play and other activities so that you can encourage their development? (As opposed to merely supervising.)

- Do the children feel secure in their surroundings so that they are not inhibited or unsure when they undertake activities?

- Are the children given enough first-hand experience of any activity and, subsequently, the opportunities to practise and so consolidate their learning?

- Finally, are the activities enjoyable, rewarding and satisfying?

IDEA

75

Maximizing the potential of ideas

We hope that we have given enough examples in other ideas to make the point that most activities and pieces of equipment can be used in many ways beyond their ordinary or orthodox function. Creativity means 'going beyond the given'. When you see the potential of something beyond its conventional use, you are giving children the opportunity to learn to do that for themselves through their own experience.

So, for instance, a clock can be utilized to do more than teach children to tell the time. Ask them to listen to the sound it makes and use this to practise rhythm, beating time, counting seconds and estimating periods of time. Use it to show angles, to illustrate left and right and the points of the compass. Talk about numbers and Roman numerals. Compare the traditional circular clock with more modern digital clocks. With older children, talk about why clocks are round, why they go up to 12. Talk about the 24-hour clock. Look at other ways of measuring time – water-clocks, hour-glasses and egg-timers, etc.

 As another example, take sand play. Look at sand that is neither very dry nor very wet. Watch sand getting wetter/drier with the children. Make landscapes featuring rivers and lakes. Look at the fluidity of sand as water is added. Hide tiny shells, sequins and other surprises in sand and get the children to sieve it to see what they can find. Encourage children to play pirates, explorers and dinosaurs.

For children to develop their insight into an object's potential, you must see it first.

IDEA 76

The importance of 'situational play'

Perhaps it's a very obvious point to make, but children's play will be very different depending on whether they have the freedom of the floor, or are sitting or standing at a table. As an experiment, put out a farmyard set on the floor and on a table and notice how the children behave.

It's likely that on the floor children will use that freedom to extend their play as they adopt lots of physical positions. They can sit, lie on their sides or backs, see the playthings from floor level (as well as the more usual bird's-eye view). Compare this with their behaviour seated at and standing around a table. Such simple observations will not only guide you to provide the play items that best suit the situation but also encourage you to explore ways of maximizing the potential of that situation.

Observing children's play

The point has been made earlier (see Idea 75) that creativity is about 'going beyond the given'. To achieve this, the 'given' must previously be explored through close observation. In other words, in order to extend children's play you must have observed children at play in a range of situations. We appreciate that record-keeping is an important part of your good practice. All too often, however, we have seen early years practitioners filling out forms and tick-sheets about a child *as that child plays*. The disadvantage of this is that the practitioner only has half an eye on the child and is mainly concerned with scribbling notes, thus missing many of the subtleties and small details of their play.

Our opinion is that the practitioner would find it more useful and enjoyable simply to watch the child and write up observations later. This approach also helps the adult to judge if, when or how far to intervene in a child's play in order to extend it. If children are playing 'Mummies and Daddies' in the home corner, drop by as a visitor. If children are sticking pegs randomly into a pegboard, suggest making patterns.

As part of your own development, play with the toys and equipment yourself. Pretend that you are 3 again and immerse yourself in play. This will help you to see the potential of the toys and to know how to join in with the children – which is important, as there is often a fine line between intervention and interference.

IDEA 78

Six super activities

These are among our all-time favourites. If you haven't run them in your setting, maybe you should give them a go soon...

- Making pancakes on Pancake Day. On the day before, we'd take some children shopping for the necessary ingredients, including a range of toppings such as orange juice, lemon juice, honey and sugar. The children would make the mix, we'd cook the pancakes and the children would choose the topping they wanted. (*Note*: This activity covers all the Early Learning Goals!)

- Marching games in the garden/playground on a cold day. Wrap them up warm and get the children to do giant-stepping, tiptoe steps, long hops, frog-leaps, star-jumps and follow-my-leader.

- Relaxation and calming with chiffon scarves or other light fabric. Get the children to move with them to gentle music, lie on the floor with the fabric over their faces and blow gently, etc. (Very soothing.)

- Bubble-painting. Supply each child with her own straw. Prepare some containers filled with liquid paint and washing-up liquid added (not too much). The child puts the straw into the paint and blows creating a 'frothy coffee' texture on the surface. Gently touch a sheet of paper to the surface to make some exquisite effects.

- Storytelling. See Ideas 82–94 and our *100 Ideas for Teaching Creative Development* for further tips. Our all-time favourite story-for-telling was 'Mr Noisy'.

- Group games. A favourite was the snail game. This is a bought game featuring some coloured wooden snails, a 'race track' and a coloured die. Children take turns to roll the die and move their snail towards the finishing line. In our version, whatever colour any child rolled, the owner of that snail would move it forward. This encouraged sharing and cooperation.

IDEA

79

An eye for safety

The safety of children touches upon all aspects of your setting and the work you do there. Risk assessments form a cumbersome bureaucratic attempt to ensure that children are safe and secure, but such a system is worthless unless you as an individual are constantly aware of the potential dangers in even the most apparently harmless activities. For instance, a worn or damaged jigsaw puzzle piece could be the source of harmful splinters.

Broadly speaking, some activities require your general supervision as a 'watchful and caring presence' in the room. Others, however, demand close supervision, where your attention and diligence must be much more finely focused. Water and sand play, small toys and beads and the use of certain equipment such as scissors fall into this category. In order to realize the importance of such alertness it's necessary to recognize the potential harm of these things and situations.

By way of developing your sensitivity to this issue, consider carrying out a safety audit of your room. This is not a 'risk assessment' in the sense that you have to think of all possible dangers attached to every activity you might conceivably do with the children, but a practical and thorough look around to spot actual or potential sources of danger.

Have things been put back on shelves properly so that they won't fall and hurt a passing child? Are door and cupboard handles at child eye level? (If so, how could this danger be rectified?) Are pieces of equipment, toys, etc. in good repair? Be aware, too, that small children like to put things in their mouths, so always have disinfectant wipes at the ready and wash plastic toys thoroughly on a regular basis.

Because these things are obvious they are sometimes forgotten, so remember to 'think safety'.

IDEA

80

Play-corner vocabulary

You may not think it appropriate to join in with the children in the play corner, but when you do, use it as an opportunity to extend and develop the play and the language that accompanies it. In other words, don't just put things out and let the children get on with it.

So, if you want to set up a garage in the play corner, equip it with a variety of tools above and beyond the most obvious ones that a mechanic would use. Tell the children the names of these tools and explain how they are used. (If you don't know, ask a mechanic!) Be aware also of the fact that words we know – such as 'mechanic' – might be a complete mystery to some children. Forge word-links where possible so that the children can appreciate the connection between mechanic and machine for instance.

If you really want to be thorough you might think about preparing a vocabulary list as well as an equipment list for a range of play-corner situations. Give some thought also as to how you might extend, link and sometimes simplify activities to cater for the different children in your setting.

IDEA 81

The journey to competence

Throughout this book we've tried to offer practical tips and techniques about how to develop your own good practice. Such advice forms the 'flesh on the bones' of certain basic principles that we feel are rooted not just in common sense but also in a vast range of educational literature about how the brain functions and how learning occurs. Understanding and accepting these principles creates a context for checking the learning value of any activities you want to run with the children. We feel that some of the most valuable insights, and the ones that inform our educational careers, include:

● The roots of the word education mean 'to draw out and rear up'. While it's necessary for us to tell and show children a great deal, true learning happens when we draw out from them (through talk and play for instance) what they understand about the world. When we acknowledge and value their emergent understanding, children are 'reared up' to be confident, creative and enthusiastic learners.

● Knowing 'how' is more important than knowing 'what'. In others words, experience is a more powerful teacher than simple knowledge. This insight is the basis of all experiential learning – *learning by doing*.

● Competence in any skill or ability is best thought of not as a goal, target or outcome, but as an ongoing journey – a process, an unfolding of potential that carries on throughout and beyond the school years. Drawing out children's ideas and helping them to learn through direct experience, walking with them on their journey to competence, forms the foundation of your good practice.

IDEA 82

The importance of story

Stories form an important part of children's experiences in all early years settings, and are universally recognized as being of immense educational value. You might give some thought as to why this is so before looking at some of our reasons:

- Stories and 'story-time' develop children's listening, concentration and memory.

- Stories create a sense of wonder (and bring opportunities for children to experience a range of other emotions).

- Stories expose children to a wide variety of different ideas, viewpoints and perspectives while offering a shared experience to the listeners.

- Stories provide information and help children to sequence events by serving as 'organizational templates' for making sense of the world (see the notion of narrative structure below).

- Stories widen children's vocabulary, not just through introducing new words, but by rehearsing different contexts in which words are used. Thus children come to understand that a word may have several meanings or many shades of meaning depending upon how it is used.

- Stories make links between the spoken and written words and between these and pictures (visual representations of ideas).

- Stories build children's understanding of narrative structure, where events have a sequence that move towards a resolution, where characters who may be good and/or evil are involved, where issues and problems are explored. etc.

- Knowledge of narrative structure generates a way of thinking about life itself, in terms of characters, chapters, beginnings and endings, resolutions, turning over a new leaf and so on.

- Stories stimulate interest in, and enjoyment of, books.

- Stories develop the imagination.

We hope you agree!

Reading and telling

We think the notion of story*telling* is important. True storytelling goes far beyond the concept of an adult sitting in front of a group of children, reading more or less verbatim from the page. If you are new to storytelling then the temptation is there to rely entirely on the book – although even at this early stage your voice and mannerisms, your whole persona, will make a huge difference to the children's experience. As your experience and confidence grow, however, we feel sure that you will use books less, or in different ways, as well as employing a much greater range of techniques and resources in your telling.

Consider how you might use the following in developing your storytelling skills:

● pre-recorded tapes/CDs with an appropriate storybook

● storyboards (that you can make yourself)

● puppets

● musical instruments

● recorded music to create mood and atmosphere and to encourage imaginative thought

● a treasure box or bag containing a range of appropriate objects

● pictures and photographs

● improvisation (making it up as you go along), either closely based on a story you know, or putting characters from different stories together to see what happens!

- asking questions that help the children to make up their own stories
- using a selection of words and pictures drawn randomly from a bag.

IDEA 84

Developing your storytelling skills

In our opinion, trying out different ways of presenting stories and relying less and less on 'verbatim reading' (using a book for support), is necessary if you want to develop your storytelling skills.

At first you may feel lost without the book in front of you – but of course you can have it nearby to refer to if necessary, or you might simply jot down key words on a piece of paper as a prompt. It also helps if you tell (as opposed to read) a story that you enjoy and one that is familiar to you. That in itself helps to build the confidence to tell. Try it out. You've got nothing to lose, and if it's a success you'll be delighted when the children ask you to 'tell it again!'

You'll also find that many children are surprised when you start a story session without a book – 'You've forgotten our book!' is a common cry. This creates the opportunity to explain to the children that a story can be told in *lots* of ways, not just through a book. This not only reassures the children but also gives them a valuable insight. Furthermore, as your own telling skills grow, the children will pick up a huge amount about effective communication – use and control of the voice, facial expression, eye-contact, body posture, involvement of the audience, mastery of the 'content' of the story through the use of pauses and silence, pace, evocation of mood and atmosphere, etc.

IDEA

85

Varying your storytelling

In the previous few ideas we have emphasized the value of story and developing a variety of techniques for telling that move you beyond the use of books. The benefits for you and the children in doing this are numerous:

● When telling (as opposed to reading) a story, don't feel you have to give the title at the start. Children enjoy guessing games. But more importantly, if the story is one they've heard before their memories will be stimulated as they search for a title they 'know they know'.

● Telling different stories, including ones that are unfamiliar to the children, will create excitement and anticipation as they try to work out what might happen next. Anticipation, incidentally, is a thinking skill that is useful in many different contexts of the children's learning.

● Children are involved more actively and positively when you talk with them and question them, rather than just reading to them.

● Using a range of media when telling stimulates the children's own questioning skills and also their abilities to attend, concentrate and invent.

IDEA 86

The story environment – the children

Listening to a story is an ability that we can cultivate in children, and one that will bring them many benefits throughout their school years and beyond. The quality of the children's experience during a storytelling session depends on many factors, all of which need to be considered by the early years practitioner beforehand.

In terms of the children themselves, are they required to sit on the floor or do they (or can they) have chairs? If they have to be on the floor, can they lie down as well as sit? For many children who are read to at home, the story session happens at bedtime. Such children may not be familiar or comfortable with sitting and may well concentrate and enjoy the story more if they can lie down.

If they have the option of lying down, is there enough space for them to move, stretch out, etc.? It's very difficult for anyone to sit or lie still for long. This is not just about being 'naturally fidgety': children react to what happens in stories and that includes moving, even to the extent of grabbing on to the person next to them at an exciting bit!

We feel it's good practice to give children the choice of sitting or lying when you want them to listen well. If children are comfortable they will be more attentive and involved in the story and can concentrate for longer. Your 'story space' should be able to accommodate this choice.

IDEA 87

The story environment – the space

Story corners, or any areas where you want children to listen well, should be comfortable, cosy and inviting. As well as the points made in Idea 86 about the children having enough room and a choice of listening positions, is the temperature right? Obviously if children are too hot or too cold they will be distracted. It's not always possible to test the temperature from your storyteller's chair. Are there draughts at floor level? Sit on the floor and find out. An open window or a door that's ajar can send cold air streaming across the floor that you might otherwise never have noticed. Also, even if the room thermometer registers an acceptable temperature, because heat rises the air might be several degrees colder where the children are sitting.

Is the story area enclosed or open, and can it be modified to suit your purposes? If the space is open, can the children see everything around them if they need to? There's nothing more distracting than something happening out of sight. The child's natural tendency (and ours too probably) is to want to know what it is! If the children can see what's going on they'll take a peek and then get back to the story.

If the story space is enclosed, our feeling is that *nothing else* should be happening in the room during story-time. Concentration is a skill that needs to be developed and cultivated. If the children are sitting in a screened-off area while other things are happening in the room then you will be undermining your own efforts in helping them to listen well.

IDEA

88

The story environment – the time

Do you routinely have your story sessions at the same time in the day? And have you explored the reasons behind this? Some early years settings slot story-time in at the end of the morning or afternoon in order to have the children all together while other staff tidy up in anticipation of parents arriving. We think this is bad practice because it is done for adults' convenience and not the quality of the children's experience.

As well as the 'distraction factor' mentioned in Idea 87, the arrival of each parent (even if they stand patiently at the door) will take children's attention away from the story. In our opinion, instead of a story session at such times, singing, group rhymes or movement activities are better suited. If you haven't done so, try story sessions at different times in the day to see what works best.

As well as the positioning of the session in the day, the length of the session itself must be considered. A number of factors are important here, including the age of the children and their ability to concentrate. Perhaps more important, though, is your confidence and experience as the teller. A good storyteller can hold children's attention for a long time and keep them fully involved.

IDEA

89

The story environment – the teller

By way of summarizing many of the points we've made about storytelling, we feel that good storytelling is:

- *Rehearsed.* You will have read the story through several times and to some extent 'made it your own'. We recommend also telling the story aloud to yourself. Stories often tell differently from the way they read.

- *Controlled.* You will have thought about the story environment from the children's point of view. You will also be in control of all the aspects of the telling itself – the pace, volume and tone of your voice, the use of tension and dramatic silence, the way you 'play' the audience by using eye-contact, gestures and so on.

- *Fresh.* You will bring that vital element of freshness to the session by telling the story as though it were new and exciting for you. If a story you've told many times before comes out now as though it's a dreary chore, the children will simply not enjoy it. However, your familiarity with the story is an advantage because, knowing what's coming yourself, you can build the children's anticipation in many subtle ways.

- *Flexible.* You will be in control of the story session and also able to accommodate children's spontaneous or impromptu comments and other unexpected factors. If there is a loud noise outside, do you ignore it or can it somehow be woven into the tale? If a child suddenly needs to visit the toilet, is this a distraction for you and the other children, or is there something you can say that will draw their attention back into the story?

- *Immersive.* 'Immersion' means the total involvement of a child in the activity in which he is engaged. When children are completely 'inside' the story (you will be too of course) then the experience will be most powerful and most beneficial to them. As well as what we have said so far, what else do you think could help to immerse children in a story?

IDEA

90

Ringing the changes

Effective and successful storytelling results from increasing self-confidence, but by the same token, trying out different ways of involving children in the experience of story will help to build your confidence and creative abilities.

Once you have a repertoire of stories that you are familiar with, and have insight into how the control of the voice makes a story more dramatic, exciting, scary, etc., you will probably be happy to try out different ways of storytelling to develop your skills even further.

Consider using just the pictures in a storybook. You can display these so that the children see the whole sequence of pictures, which act as a rich visual reference to the tale itself. If the children already know the story, the pictures aid memory and stimulate discussion of further details. If they do not know the story, use the pictures to make up a plot that works.

Or you can show the pictures one at a time as the story unfolds. The visual will help to prompt your memory and perhaps encourage you to add improvised details in the telling. It also serves to focus the children's attention as they listen.

Another use of pictures is to cut out a selection from magazines and comics. Use them in the ways noted above to adapt stories the children already know, or create new stories.

Using musical instruments with stories

Introducing 'sound effects' to stories adds a delightful new dimension and also creates the opportunity to develop children's auditory abilities – their ability to notice different qualities of a sound, to be aware of similarities and differences between sounds, and to match sounds with verbal descriptions. This in turn stimulates the search for vocabulary and provides you with the opportunity to introduce the children to new sound words.

In the story of 'The Three Billy Goats Gruff', for instance, as the goats arrive at the bridge ask the children what kind of sound the smallest goat would make as he crosses. Share ideas, but also have some instruments to hand so that the children can listen and then decide which sound works best. We found that a tulip-block was the usual choice. Then ask about the middle goat (a tambour makes an appropriate sound), and then the big goat (perhaps a drum).

You don't have to limit yourself to musical instruments of course. Use all kinds of objects to find out what sounds they make – the clip-clop of shoes, the clink-clank of tin cans (made safe), the crackle of cellophane, etc.

Finger-puppets and story

Finger-puppets add colour, movement and fun to a storytelling session. When the children use finger-puppets too you have added a kinaesthetic dimension to their experience, which will also help to hold their attention and remember the tale in greater detail.

Sets of finger-puppets that match particular stories can be bought these days, but helping the children to make their own is enjoyable and educationally more worthwhile. Children can choose the characters they want from a selection of magazines, comics and pictures. We've found that comics are especially useful. The children cut out their chosen pictures and stick them on card. Sometimes it's possible to cut two holes in the picture so a child can push his fingers through to use as the character's legs. Otherwise, stick the picture to two rectangles of card that have been taped together, leaving the bottom edges untaped so the child can push his finger inside to support the finger-puppet in that way. You can of course always run a bigger and more elaborate art activity by making the puppets out of felt or other fabric that's sewn rather than glued.

It's preferable that every child in the group has a finger-puppet of his own. Be prepared to modify the story to accommodate this. Finger-puppets need not just be characters in the story, but might be trees, clouds, the sun, moon and stars or other objects that are important to the plot. Using many finger-puppets in a way that involves all the children moves the story towards a dramatization that the children will enjoy very much, through their active role in the telling.

IDEA 93

Objects from a bag or treasure box

Once you feel comfortable telling a story without a book and feel able to improvise, try inviting the children to draw objects from a bag or treasure box to make up new stories or variations on familiar ones.

If you decide to try this, initially select objects that fit with a story you already know. At least then you'll have some narrative framework to support you in thinking of new ideas. Beyond this, consider how different objects might be incorporated into a story. At first glance, a crocodile, polar bear and kangaroo might seem to work well in a story that will be about animals. But unless the story is a 'nonsense tale' or about a zoo it's not likely you'd find these animals together.

There's nothing wrong with nonsense stories of course, although you probably wouldn't want every story to be one. Note also that children can get very excitable when making up such tales as they let their imaginations run wild. You must know how to calm such a group and/or bring the story back on a more reasonable track. It would be a shame for the session to fall apart in chaos if it means that you are less likely to try it again and give the children another chance.

Tip: If you make up a bag of objects that relate to a familiar story, try first picking an object that doesn't immediately give the game away. For 'Goldilocks and the Three Bears', for instance, instead of a bear, pick out the number 3, or a bowl or a chair. This creates the elements of surprise and anticipation and gives children the chance to have a range of ideas before the story proper gets going.

IDEA 94

Story-making

We hope we've said enough in this section to convince you of the many great benefits of storytelling with children. All of it serves as a precursor to helping children create their own stories, which in turn will be of immense use to them throughout their education. Creating stories presupposes some understanding of narrative structure that will help the children to interpret and analyse language when they are older. You are also cultivating in them a love of stories which hopefully they will pass on to *their* children in time.

A simple way of working with children to make up new stories is to select words and pictures from a bag. However, it will be a real test of your own and the children's imaginations. The best stories are a reasoned integration of ideas; in other words they have a definite narrative structure. Simply letting a child's imagination run away with him is not the same as creative thinking and effective story-making. So, plan such a session carefully, taking into account the particular children with whom you will be working.

Some children will come out with the most unlikely, outrageous and even sometimes provocative ideas. There's no need to judge, deny or discard such ideas. Rather, we have found it useful to explain to a child that *anything that's put into a story needs to be there for a good reason that will help the story to be the best it can be.*

We recommend that you establish this principle from the outset. So if for instance you are making up a story about a lonely old lady who takes in a lodger and you ask what that lodger might be like and a child blurts out 'A lion!', apply the principle. If we use that idea, why would a lion want to stay in an old lady's house and why would the old lady want to accept the lion as a lodger?

An imaginative child might say 'He wants to eat the old lady!' Apply the principle. Why would the lion go to the trouble of calling at the old lady's house when he could choose anybody off the street? And why is the lion wandering around loose in the first place?

Use your judgement in how far you keep questioning the child to look for reasonable explanations. But be sure to establish the point that even in fantastical stories everything happens for reasons that the reader will find acceptable.

IDEA 95

Asking questions in story-making

When you ask children questions as you make up stories you are modelling a number of educationally useful techniques:

- You are teaching children about the importance of questions in discovering information.

- You are showing children that there are many kinds of questions and that often there are many possible answers to a question.

- You are valuing enquiry as a learning strategy and implicitly pointing out that it's OK not to know the answers at the beginning.

Also, when you ask questions, you have a great degree of control over the children's thinking and their verbal responses. Two useful questioning techniques you can use when helping children to create stories are the use of closed questions and 'the six big important questions':

- Closed questions demand 'yes or no' answers, or an otherwise limited choice of response. So you can say, 'Shall we make the story start in the night-time or the daytime?' A vote will settle the matter, or you might explore the reasons for choosing a night-time beginning as opposed to a daytime opening scene. Closed questions focus attention, but can act as a springboard into open questioning. If you ask, 'Is the lion at the start of our story unhappy?', and the children decide yes, you can then ask, 'Why might he be unhappy?' The range of responses you get will generate further ideas you can then weave into the tale.

- The 'six big important questions' are 'where', 'when', 'what', 'who', 'why' and 'how'. Use these as appropriate to generate more details, to explore how different parts of the story link, to discuss the motives of the character (why they do what they do) and to create a robust plot structure.

IDEA

96

Using stories to explore sensitive issues

This idea raises the question of whether, or how far, it is part of an early years practitioner's role to discuss sensitive issues such as bullying, bereavement, race, disability and more with the children. Our view is that since the setting is there to further the children's education, these matters need to be addressed, if not as a matter of course then certainly in response to any child's queries about them. Policy decisions need to be made and all staff should have ways of broaching these subjects with the children.

Books are a wonderful way of helping children to understand and deal with sensitive issues. Our view is that even if some children haven't experienced bullying or 'being different', they should know that these things can happen. Furthermore, books can, and often do, portray positive outcomes, and their characters create a sense of shared experience. A lonely child can feel kinship with a character who is lonely in a story.

The 'positive messages' in books need not be overt or preachy, and, in fact, we think it isn't vital that children even realize that the issue is being explored. In our experience, most children are very accepting of other people and usually don't display the prejudiced attitudes of some adults. So when you read the *Elmer the Elephant* stories with a group the children, they might never notice or be troubled by the fact that Elmer is different from the other elephants. But these stories will form part of the children's understanding of the world and offer implicit guidance as to how they can behave.

Books, then, offer a valuable means of introducing children to concepts, feelings, dilemmas and resolutions that they may well encounter in their everyday lives.

IDEA
97

Setting up a book corner

We feel that a book corner is a vitally important part of any early years setting. A book corner is not a story corner, but rather an area where children can go and sit (or lie down) and experience books for themselves. Ideally, a book corner will be a quiet and comfortable area with cushions, a couple of chairs or a settee, and an inviting selection of books.

If you intend to set up or 'refresh' a book corner in your setting, it is important to put yourself at the child's eye level. What do you see? Is the corner an inviting space that makes you want to sit there and explore? Are the books clean and otherwise well looked after? (We'll look at this in more detail in the next idea.) And are they attractively displayed? It's better to have fewer books face out on the shelves than a greater number standing edge on. Finally, does the timetable and ethos of the setting allow children some freedom to come and go as they please in the book corner and not to feel rushed when they are there?

Children need to learn that books are valuable. Getting the most out of books is a skill. Telling the children so won't be enough; they have to experience it for themselves and there is no better way than giving them access to a cosy book corner.

IDEA 98

Choosing the books for a book corner

Particular titles can (and should) be discussed at staff meetings, and we feel it is good practice to allow all staff the chance to choose books for a book corner. What's most important is that even if the books are bought second-hand, from a charity shop or jumble sale for instance, they should be clean and in good repair. If tatty books are put in the book corner, children will not learn to respect and look after them.

When you are searching for second-hand books, check to make sure the pages are not torn or heavily repaired with sticky tape, and that they have not been scribbled in. Select a good variety of books that you think will have wide appeal. Do you intend to feature factual books as well as story and picture books in the book corner? Will you display books by theme? And will these be related to the children's ongoing work or be completely unrelated? You may choose to buy puzzle and wordsearch books. Explain that these are different and can be written and drawn in: attach a pencil for children to use just with those particular books. Refresh displays often.

As you build your stock, be sure to show children how to handle books. Discourage children from treating books disrespectfully. Model good behaviour by picking up any dropped books from the floor, then ask the children to do the same. Play your part in keeping the book corner a place where the children want to be.

IDEA
99

A listening frame of mind

Before the storyteller Pomme Clayton begins to tell her tales, she sets a colourful piece of fabric in front of her and places a range of small musical instruments upon it. Before each story, Pomme picks up a little bell or a triangle or a penny whistle and sounds it – 'So you have your listening ears ready'. As the session progresses the audience already have their listening ears ready even as Pomme begins to choose the next instrument. They have learned to associate this little ritual with good listening and the anticipation of a tale about to be told.

This technique is called *anchoring*. An anchor, in this sense, is a link that you make in the children's minds between a behaviour you want them to do (in this case, good sitting and listening) and something that you have direct control over – the tinging of a triangle or the peep of a whistle, etc. Anchoring techniques are powerful and from the practitioner's point of view, form an elegant and respectful way of managing your setting.

Anchors are very varied. Using a musical instrument is an auditory anchor. Story and book corners are spatial anchors. Children come to associate those particular areas with all the pleasures that go with listening to, handling and looking at books. Particular book covers can act as visual anchors – the mere sight of that book can evoke memories and feelings in a child that he associates with his previous experiences of it.

In these basic ways, anchoring can enhance the positive effects you want to create through allowing children to experience books and stories.

IDEA

100

A final thought

It is our hope that the insights, tips and techniques in this book will help you to develop your own good practice, or offer concise advice that you can pass on to others who are not as experienced as yourself. Of course, we have only scratched the surface of what there is to know, and even after many years of working with young children we realize – as you surely do – that there is always more to learn.

But whether you are new to early years education, or count yourself as a 'veteran', the best practice depends as much on your own confidence, self-assurance and ability to think calmly and clearly as it does on how many teaching techniques you have mastered. What if a child hurt herself badly in the playground and you had to look after the rest of the children, perhaps a large group of them, while other staff dealt with the injury or phoned an ambulance? What would you say and do so that those children in your care remained calm and felt safe?

Heaven forbid that such a thing should ever happen. But it's crises such as these as well as the day-to-day joys of working in early years education that is the real test of how much we have learned.

Self-Evaluation Form

Level of awareness and understanding	A	B	C	D	E
Health and Safety: Shows awareness of safety hazards.					
Can carry out H&S policies and procedures relating to: ● children ● equipment ● environment					
Can carry out procedures necessary to ensure the safety and security of: ● children ● equipment ● pets ● premises ● personal belongings					
Can follow procedures to deal with: ● accidents ● emergencies ● fire-drills ● administration of medicines and drugs ● arrival of children ● collection of children ● visitors					
Cleaning and Maintenance: Shows a responsible attitude towards cleaning and care of equipment.					
Can carry out cleaning and maintenance duties in respect of: ● top room ● front room ● middle room ● art room					

Level of awareness and understanding	A	B	C	D	E
• toilet area					
• cloakroom/corridors/utility area					
• serving of snacks					
• serving of meals					
• clearing away after snacks/meals					
• cleaning tables/washing up					
• garden/play area					
• pets					
• equipment					
Personal and Social Development:					
Shows a cheerful and welcoming disposition to:					
• children					
• parents					
• other adults					
• students					
• visitors					
• other professionals					
Can establish and maintain effective relationships with:					
• children					
• parents/carers					
• colleagues					
• students					
Can work cooperatively with colleagues:					
• offer support					
• give encouragement					
Can be a positive role model for:					
• children					
• parents/carers					
• students					
• visitors					
Can carry out daily/timetable routines:					

Level of awareness and understanding	A	B	C	D	E
Can follow rules and regulations with regard to:					
● policy documents					
● social services requirements					
● fire department requirements					
● environmental health requirements					
● food hygiene requirements					
Can use the telephone effectively to:					
● make relevant calls					
● receive calls/take messages accurately					
Can use the intercom system effectively:					
● to receive messages					
● to give messages					
● for fire-drill procedures					
Can take responsibility for stock					
Has produced a creative activity folder					
Has produced an anthology of poems, songs and rhymes					
Can produce child observations accurately					
Can produce a child study in detail					
Has devised and produced materials to assist in:					
● telling stories					
● group games					
● rhymes and songs					
● discussions					
● topics and themes					
Has devised and produced a variety of visual aids:					
● story boards					
● finger-puppet(s)					
● jigsaw/model (or similar)					
● game/picture cards					
Can devise activities in various areas of the curriculum:					
● creative play					

Level of awareness and understanding	A	B	C	D	E
• imaginative play					
• outdoor play					
• matching/sorting games					
• coordination skills					
• simple science					
• water/sand play					
• music					
• pre-reading skills					
• numeracy skills					
Can assist and supervise children off nursery premises: • outings in minibus/trips with parents • walks locally • parties/carnival and related activities					
Shows an understanding of observing and record-keeping:					
Child Development:					
Has gained an understanding of what to expect from a child of: • up to 6 months • 6–12 months • up to 2 years • 2–3 years • 3–4 years • 4–5 years • over 5 years • special needs • other culture					
Can identify the needs of children and carry out the tasks required for their personal care and hygiene with regard to: • dressing • washing • toileting • personal hygiene • snacks/mealtimes					

Level of awareness and understanding	A	B	C	D	E
Able to identify when a child is ready to take on for his/herself some of the tasks above:					
Can show an understanding of and deal with the needs of children regarding: ● general development ● manipulative skills ● gross motor skills ● listening skills ● concentration skills ● emotional development ● social development ● language/communication skills					
Can show an understanding of and deal with the particular needs of children with: ● emotional problems ● social problems ● physical disabilities ● mental disabilities ● 'settling in' problems					
Can hold attention and maintain concentration of children in group activities: ● story ● group games ● drama ● music ● group round games					
Can organize and participate with the children in: ● board-games ● singing activities ● music activities ● gross motor activities ● outdoor activities ● drama and movement ● imaginative play					